WHITE NEGROES

WHITE NEGROES

WHEN CORNROWS WERE IN VOGUE ...
AND OTHER THOUGHTS
ON CULTURAL APPROPRIATION

LAUREN MICHELE JACKSON

BEACON PRESS, BOSTON

BEACON PRESS
Boston, Massachusetts
www.beacon.org

Beacon Press books
are published under the auspices of
the Unitarian Universalist Association of Congregations.

22 21 20 19   8 7 6 5 4 3 2 1

This book is printed on acid-free paper that meets the uncoated paper
ANSI/NISO specifications for permanence as revised in 1992.

Text design and composition by Kim Arney

Some of this work appeared in different form in
Model View Culture and *Essence*.

Library of Congress Cataloging-in-Publication Data

Names: Jackson, Lauren Michele, author.
Title: White Negroes : when cornrows were in vogue . . . and other
thoughts on cultural appropriation / Lauren Michele Jackson.
Description: Boston, Massachusetts : Beacon Press, [2019] |
Includes bibliographical references and index.
Identifiers: LCCN 2019010980 (print) | LCCN 2019980313 (ebook) |
ISBN 9780807011805 (hardcover) | ISBN 9780807011980 (ebook)
Subjects: LCSH: African Americans in popular culture. | Popular
culture—United States. | Cultural appropriation—United States.
Classification: LCC E185.625 .J328 2019 (print) | LCC E185.625 (ebook) |
DDC 306.0973—dc23
LC record available at https://lccn.loc.gov/2019010980
LC ebook record available at https://lccn.loc.gov/2019980313

To Mommy and Tom,
who gave me language,
with love

So there was a new breed of adventurers, urban adventurers who drifted out at night looking for action with a black man's code to fit their facts. The hipster had absorbed the existentialist synapses of the Negro, and for practical purposes could be considered a white Negro.

—NORMAN MAILER, "The White Negro:
Superficial Reflections on the Hipster"

A reiteration of the obvious is never wasted on the oblivious.

—PERCIVAL EVERETT, *Erasure*

CONTENTS

WHITE NEGROES

Appropriation and American Mythmaking

Conscience, it has been said, makes cowards of us all.[1]

"**A**ppropriation" gets a bad rap. The word, centuries old, denotes an act of transport—some item or motif or a bit of property changing hands. An artist might appropriate an ancient symbol in a painting or a government might appropriate monies through taxes to fund public education. Taking only the root of the word, the meaning seems clear. To *make something appropriate* for another context. In some circles, the word is still used this way. But colloquially? Not so much.

The debate over cultural appropriation rages on. It was not too many years ago that a certain former Disney star suited in unicorn pajamas rattled her waist in an online video that went viral, prompting America to find language and meaning for what exactly was happening, the language with which to encounter this white girl who so loved black dance.

Versions of this debate have risen up repeatedly. The practice of repurposing culture is as old as culture itself, and America has been *making* other cultures *appropriate* to its amusement and ambitions since the very beginning. "You've taken my blues and gone," Langston Hughes laments in the opening of his 1940 poem "Note on Commercial Theatre."[2] In the 1920s, the poet, playwright, and author observed the great promise in the recognized gatherings of Negro artists making Negro art. Nearly two decades later, he frets over the problem that Negro art no longer needs Negroes to sell, those ole blues sung "on Broadway" and "in Hollywood Bowl."[3]

1

I recall a similar anxiety emanating from the pop music takeover of Eminem. At the 2000 MTV Video Music Awards (VMAs), the rapper, sporting close-cut bleached-blond hair, entered the theater in a white "wife beater" (offensive, if not inaccurate) and loose gray sweatpants, trailed by dozens of white close-cut bleached-blond look-alikes. The performance was simple, yet clever and effective, and still memorable within the history of an awards show that only recently has failed to diagnose the culture. At the time, Eminem appeared to be the portent of hip-hop's future—artists, critics, and other protectors of the genre worried about the next coming of Elvis, worried that Eminem might catalyze a transformation of rap similar to what long ago happened to rock and roll, and to jazz before that. They weren't so wrong. Thirteen years later, the VMA for Best Hip-Hop Video was awarded to a white anti-hip-hop rap duo from Seattle named Macklemore and Ryan Lewis. Those same 2013 VMAs invited Robin Thicke and Miley Cyrus to jerk and jive to the riff of a song that would later pay court-ordered royalties to Marvin Gaye's estate for borrowing without permission.

National dialogue on appropriation extends beyond the boundaries of popular music. From Halloween costumes to Cinco de Mayo parties to the Washington Redskins to decorative bindis and other music festival fashion, the new millennium and an avowedly more conscious generation of people is tasked with taking seriously all kinds of cultural masquerade. Yet the more popular—and accusatory—the word "appropriation" has become, the fewer people seem willing to understand the meaning behind it. Where it briefly seemed obvious that dressing up as a person of another race to the point of stereotype is *not okay*, as I write this, the country is in the midst of forgiving and actively forgetting the surfaced photograph of a state governor costumed in either blackface or Klan robes. (The governor refuses to disclose which partygoer in the photo is he.) After years of being chastised for wearing sombreros and Native-like headdresses, white people feel indignant. They are paranoid that people of color see appropriation in everything.

Appropriation is everywhere, and is also inevitable. Appropriation, for better and worse, cannot stop. So long as peoples interact with other peoples, by choice or by force, cultures will intersect and mingle and graft onto each other. We call hip-hop a black thing and it is, indeed, *a black thing*, that *also* emerged in neighborhoods where black and brown people homegrown and from the South, from the islands, melded together to produce the music of their experiences in shared poverty and community. Early rap was itself an appropriation of another generation's sound—funk, soul, disco—repurposed for something different and new. Rap also revolutionized the lively form of appropriation known as sampling, a means of incorporating the past, the recent past, and other genres to make timeless music. "I have all of Billy Joel's shit in my iPod," said the legendary Grandmaster Caz in a 2007 interview with RapReviews.com, also citing Simon and Garfunkel as lyrical influences.[4] The idea that any artistic or cultural practice is closed off to outsiders at any point in time is ridiculous, especially in the age of the internet.

Most everyday acts of appropriation, done unconsciously, escape our notice: the word that works itself into your speech because your best friend sprinkles every other phrase with it and where they got it from they don't even know; a new style you have grown into without thought, without a specific icon in mind, by just going with the flow of fashion; some recipe from Pinterest or your favorite food blog that advertises itself as nothing more than chicken casserole, made with ingredients and techniques that don't, to you, recall any culture in particular; the yoga pose you sink into after a workout; the way you shimmy when your favorite song comes on. Said the eminent cultural theorist Homi K. Bhabha, in an *Artforum* roundtable on the subject, "We can never quite control these acts and their signification. They exceed intention."[5]

Which returns us to the contention at the heart of the matter: If appropriation is everywhere and everyone appropriates all the time, why does any of this matter?

The answer, in a word: power.

Leading discussions about appropriation have been limited to debates about freedom and choice, when everyone should be talking about power. The act of cultural transport is not in itself an ethical dilemma. Appropriation can often be a means of social and political repair. The foil to assimilation for so many people America puts in danger is the appropriation of normative values with a twist. Examples include cakewalking on the old plantation, extravagant realness in the ballroom, poetic verse mastered and improved upon by the descendants of those beaten or worse for the crime of literacy. Ask any book of poems by Paul Laurence Dunbar or Gwendolyn Brooks or Terrance Hayes how insurgently wonderful literature can be when black poets experiment with the forms at their disposal, even the ones that come from Europe. When the oppressed appropriate from the powerful, it can be very special indeed.

And yet.

When the powerful appropriate from the oppressed, society's imbalances are exacerbated and inequalities prolonged. In America, white people hoard power like Hungry Hungry Hippos. "One cannot understand American capitalism either historically or in its current configuration," says political scientist Michael Dawson, "without understanding the profound role that the racial order has had in shaping capitalism in the United States, key institutions such as markets, and the state itself." In the history of problematic appropriation in America, we could start with the land and crops and cuisine commandeered from Native peoples along with the mass expropriation of the labor of the enslaved. The tradition lives on. The things black people make with their hands and minds, for pay and for the hell of it, are exploited by companies and individuals who offer next to nothing in return. White people are not penalized for flaunting black culture—they are rewarded for doing so, financially, artistically, socially, and intellectually. For a white person, seeing, citing, and compensating black people, however, has no such reward and may actually prove risky. "After all," says another eminent critic, the cultural theorist Lauren Berlant, "the American Dream does not allow a lot of time for curiosity about people it is not convenient or productive to have curiosity about."[6]

The disparity in power between white and black in America is more severe than anyone can imagine from their own income bracket. According to a 2018 report by the Samuel DuBois Cook Center on Social Equity at Duke University, "Black households hold less than seven cents on the dollar compared to white households."[7] Framed another way in the same report, "A white household living near the poverty line typically has about $18,000 in wealth, while black households in similar economic straits typically have a median wealth near *zero. This means that many black families have a negative net worth*" (emphasis in original). The research also found

- Black households with a college-educated breadwinner hold less wealth than white families whose breadwinners do not have a high school diploma.
- White households with unemployed breadwinners have a higher net worth than black households whose breadwinners work full-time.
- Controlled for income, black families save at a higher rate than their white counterparts and spend less than whites.
- White single-parent households have over double the net worth of two-parent black households; and single white women with children possess wealth equal to single black women without children.

These figures ought to be staggering. They should be made plain and visible everywhere, as profuse and common as the severe inequality quantified. They should be posted on the sliding doors of every Trader Joe's in the nation, pinned on every campus corkboard, memorized by every magnet school child until members of the next generation of American overachievers know how little merit and achievement matter in this country. Contrary to myths that say *if only black folks did right*—saved money, went to college, got married, started a business—nothing is as predictive of success in America as being born white. In fact, as the report concludes, "There are no actions that black Americans can take unilaterally that will have much of an effect on reducing the racial wealth gap." Another report, published by the Institute for Policy Studies in 2016, found that if current trends continue, the average black family won't reach the amount of wealth white families own *today* for another 228 years.[8] This is reality. This is America.

The enormity of this wealth gap is exacerbated by the gap between who is allowed to thrive off intellectual property and who is prevented from doing so by this nation's hysterical, driving compulsion to own and regulate all things black. From dabbing to "squad," collards to street wear, babywearing to voguing to EDM, jazz to "lit" to "slay" to durags; from

Timbs to Kimberlé W. Crenshaw's "intersectionality," it is destiny that black insights will be grasped by white hands, passed along from the edgy to the not-so-edgy, till everyone joins in, even the racists. This can take a long time, decades even, though the internet lights a fire under the timeline. When it's time to pay the piper, however—that is, give credit where it's due—somehow the accolades land in the lap of somebody white, or at least someone who is not black. The contradiction is what's meant by the adage made famous by Paul Mooney: "Everybody wanna be a nigga, but don't nobody wanna be a nigga," an ambivalent turn of phrase. Everybody wants the insurgence of blackness with the wealth of whiteness. Everybody wants to be cool without fearing for their lives. They want blackness only as a suggestion, want to remain nonblack, keep centuries of subjection and violence at bay with the prefix *non-* firmly in place. When appropriative gestures flow to the powerful, amnesia follows. When culture is embraced and its people discarded, it's too easy to trick the country into believing somebody white started it all. Nor does the American Dream offer incentive to investigate the possibility that it might be otherwise.

This is a book about black aesthetics without black people. Each of the following essays takes up an area of popular culture, each curious in its own way about the desire for black culture by people who are not black. It's a strange half-life indeed, blackness in decay without its people. There's the dead black boy made art at the 2017 Whitney Biennial, the fall of a Southern cuisine queen named Paula Deen, there's Marc Jacobs, Christina Aguilera, the Kardashians, the Women's March. Mostly, though, the figures exposed are us, consumers of culture regularly bamboozled by the tireless process of American mythmaking.

To anyone confused about it all, I hope that I may be of service in enlightenment.

To those who count themselves allies, may these essays make you a little less sure of yourselves.

To those *who been knew*, may you revel in the wonder of what people like us have made out of this dull, dull world.

PART I

Sound and Body

CHAPTER 1

The Pop Star

Swinging and Singing

A black head was cautiously protruded from the shrubbery, and a
black voice—if such a description be allowable—addressed him:—
"Is dat you, Doctuh Miller?"
"Yes. Who are you, and what's the trouble?"

A 2002 music video is set in a late-'70s New York City ghetto, though it may just as well be anytime in Langston Hughes's "Darkness, USA." On a graffitied street, children frolic in the spray of a hijacked hydrant that soaks the pavement. It is summer—a weekend, likely, but perhaps not; after all, unemployment has climbed to a high, leaving people in neighborhoods like this one without much to do besides loiter and watch one another. From one story up, two young men toss water balloons that splash beneath the tires of a bronze Cadillac idling by, disturbing the women who've made the stoop their beauty shop. A walking fro on lanky legs waltzes past, boom box to his ear. Others bounce on piled-up mattresses. B-boys gyrate against artist Keith Haring's infamous orange figures, re-made in blue. The mural spells out a cry: "Crack is wack."

The people here are diverse in a way that signals their unique sameness. They double-Dutch on a crowded sidewalk. They jaywalk, dap, push shopping carts, wear Kangol hats, wifebeaters, gold chains, candy-pink earrings, tracksuits, white socks pulled way above the ankle. They come in deep, deep browns, burnished bronzes, golds, and yellows—but one individual stands apart from the rest.

She, too, is brown, if a bit brighter, a bit lighter, a touch more peachy than sun-kissed. She wears the socks, too, just below her knee, with three lilac stripes, slid into purple plastic pumps to match the rest of the skin-tight ensemble. She also drips gold: chains, necklaces, a pair of hoops in each ear. Her jet-black hair curls around heavily kohled eyes, baby-pink lips, pencil-thin brows. On top sits a cap—also purple—that reads "Lady C" in cursive script. The *C* stands for Christina. But she's not the version we're used to.

This is Christina Aguilera, *stripped*—so states the title of her second album. From 2002, *Stripped*, and the era that followed its release, would see the pop darling undergo a transformation of aesthetic, sonic, and ethnic proportions. She was not the only one, nor the first, but this was her time to shine. *Stripped* was an opportunity for a whole new self, a more "real" self, under a new name with an ego to match—Xtina.

Xtina first unveiled herself with "Dirrty," a gritty-pop-crunk hit accompanied by an appropriately inappropriate greased-up slickshow of a music video. It prophesied the years to follow—chaps, sweat, ratty hair, and booty poppin' over a thumping, bass-laden beat.* By the time the video for "Can't Hold Us Down"—the one set in the unidentified brown and black barrio in late-'70s New York City—was released (featuring rap supreme Lil' Kim), audiences knew what the *Stripped* moment was all about. Christina's pipes could still sing the house down, but the time for innuendo about genies and friction was over. Xtina was explicit. She was tan. She was pierced. She was dirty. She was sorta, almost, *black*. Certainly blacker than ever before.

Like so many late-'90s pop heavyweights, including Britney Spears, the Southern sweetheart who would become her biggest rival, Christina boasted appearances on both *Star Search* and *Mickey Mouse Club* by the time she was a teen. As she would later tell the likes of *Rolling Stone* and the *New York Times*, the music of Christina's childhood was a bit unconventional,

---

*"Dirrty" began its life as "Let's Get Dirty (I Can't Get in da Club)," the lead single off rapper Redman's 2001 album *Malpractice*. The song was adopted with few changes for Christina's *Stripped*. Redman was added as a featured artist on the song.

at least for a white (European-Ecuadorian) kid in the Pennsylvania sub-urbs. While many Gen X'ers and older millennials made memories to the sounds of "dad rock" bands such as the Eagles, Van Halen, Boston, et al., Christina and her grandmother "would travel to Pittsburgh to scour rec-ord shops for those 'nitty-gritty' soul and blues numbers," she told *Rolling Stone* in 2006—learning from artists such as Billie Holiday, Otis Redding, Pearl Bailey, and Stevie Wonder.[1]

These influences can be felt in the very first handful of notes that launched her career. On *Star Search*, at nine years old, Christina (or "Christine Aquilero," as mispronounced by Ed McMahon) performed "A Sunday Kind of Love," a sultry '40s number cowritten by the jazz legend Louis Prima. Her rendition of the song was the latest in a tradition that included performances by Fran Warren, Ella Fitzgerald, the Harptones, Hank Jones, Dinah Washington, and Etta James. By contrast, fellow *Star Search* alums Britney and Justin Timberlake opted for country, with the Judds' "Love Can Build a Bridge" and Alan Jackson's "Love's Got a Hold on You," respectively.

"At that age, I sang songs meant for older people," Christina told *W Magazine* in 2011.[2] "That fit my personality—I had pain to sing about."[3] On the 1989-to-1996 revival of *The Mickey Mouse Club*, Christina was the little girl with the big voice, lending her talents to Aretha's "Think," Whit-ney's "I Have Nothing," and Toni's "Another Sad Love Song." Besides a divinely bestowed ability to take 'em to church, these numbers showcased a young talent whose vocal instincts emerged from another tradition, an-other culture of vocal performance. Christina's nickname was Mini Diva. The copious belts, runs, and growls that would later distinguish her from pop peers began as a testament to an industry where diva-isms ruled and there was no time for timid notes. Where par meant glamour and excess—musically speaking, but also elsewhere—showboating was merely a sign of pride in one's work. This was the sonic world black music built.

Ever since Robert "Vanilla Ice" Van Winkle and Mark "Marky Mark" Wahlberg flipped the script with funky fresh rhymes—nay, sooner, ever since Elvis Presley swiveled America into this *hip* thing called rock and roll; wait, even sooner, since adventurous white musicians began fiddling with a thing the folks back home called blues—there's been a need to reckon with what happens when black sounds come out of white artists. "The materials of the blues were not available to the white American, even though some strange circumstance might prompt him to look for them," wrote the poet and critic (among many other things) LeRoi Jones (later Amiri Baraka), in his 1963 classic *Blues People: Negro Music in White America.*[4] For Jones, "the idea of a white blues singer" was a "violent contradiction of terms." Jones tells the history of American music that, much like America itself, would not—could not—exist without black people. Most Americans of any color are familiar with and perhaps even tired of the tale of how rock and roll went white, even as the memory of Presley remains an inexhaustible source of cross-cultural fascination. Appropriation not only put the switch in Elvis's hips but also birthed the many musical movements before him and after—many still enjoyed today and many lost in archaism. Ragtime, Dixieland, bebop, any and all forms of jazz and country and soul and rhythm and blues—American music, whether it wants to or not, evinces the whoop, the whisper, the whole existence of black America. The blues, as told by Baraka, is/are not just a genre of music with set rhythms and patterns, but the lithe choreography known to those in America born to got to stay ready. As Baraka knew, black American life is movement, a living verb: we swing, we get hip, *we real cool we*. The white American, meanwhile, stands close by and observes—ready to transform life into style and profit, a process Baraka calls "the cultural lag."

But truly the lag belonged to black America. In relief against give or take four hundred years that divide black folks from the full fruits of labor juts the mighty history of musical reproduction, which papers over the diverse reality of music made in America. Over eighty years before Christina and her pussy posse "take on a gang of guys in New York's Lower East Side," black America was playing catch-up for the right to vocalize its own music.* The writer John Jeremiah Sullivan sets the scene:

---

*As put by director David LaChapelle in a 2003 interview with MTV News.

If we hear a blues queen singing on the phonograph, she will be not Mamie or Bessie or Ma, but Nora Bayes, aka Dora Goldberg, a Jewish girl from Illinois. . . . Or else she is Marion Harris, a white teenager from Indiana, from a minuscule place on the Ohio River called Pigeon Township (though she told people she came from the other side of the river, in Kentucky—it sounded better).[5]

Sullivan transports us back to the proto-blues decades between post–Civil War Reconstruction and World War I, a time when the foremost vocal talents on the blues scene were "all white girls."[6] A time when the incredible Mamie Smith gets the song "Crazy Blues" only because a Jewish girl from Connecticut—Sophie Tucker—called in sick. Where the black and genuine Kentuckian Sara Martin is introduced as "the black Sophie Tucker."

Nothing has ever stopped white people from trying to find that elusive blues—to tragic but as often thrilling results. The best and worst of the sounds produced since "Yankee Doodle" are an amalgamation on par with the Western world's reluctantly creole history: from blues to jazz to funk to disco to country to R&B to rock to rap and pop. Past Elvis, neither the English rock band the Clash nor the American rock star Bruce Springsteen could exist without the well-established borrowing that brought black music to their doors. The legendary rock critic Lester Bangs has likened the Clash to a "righteous minstrel," writing that the band made "rock capable of making a bow to black forms without smearing on the blackface."[7] Less than a year after the Clash's debut, Springsteen released one of his best (depending on who you ask) albums, *Darkness on the Edge of Town*. Thinking on the period after *Born to Run*, Springsteen says, "I began to listen seriously to country music around this time."[8] Though Springsteen is often aligned with a very white working-class tradition, "the far more appropriate—or at least coequal—lineage would be Sam Cooke, Smokey Robinson, and James Brown," says historian Jefferson Cowie.[9] Under Springsteen, the Motown song "Dancing in the Street" transforms into "Racing in the Street"—shifting from a call to freedom and whimsy to something much more desperate, capturing the bounded dreams of white working-class men. After Springsteen, the Martha and the Vandellas hit, cowritten by Marvin Gaye, is memorialized by the quirky dance moves of two other fabulous white men: David Bowie and Mick Jagger. None of this is coincidence. They all bet on black music and won, seizing commercial successes and that even more cherished prize, rock renown.

The transfer of black aesthetics to white bodies and voices, however, does not always yield transformative moments worthy of giddy remembrance. Whether for pleasure or profit or both, black music's present is regularly scraped and pasted onto white and nonblack figures who waddle their awkward forms back and forth across a worldwide stage. Sometimes the right person comes around with the right footing and a sweet voice to make something magical—Amy Winehouse, Lana Del Rey, and JC Chasez come to mind. More often, though, there's a slight discomfort, the slick dread that something has been misplaced, a track off its rail that at any moment might lead to a fiery end to us all. In 2002, Christina was a little bit of both.

It looked like a Celebrity Deathmatch for the ages," wrote music critic Josh Kun halfway through the summer of 2003:

> Christina Aguilera (half-Latina, half-suburban Pittsburgh, armed with Mariah-grade pipes and plenty of 'tude) versus Britney Spears (the quasi-innocent Louisiana Lolita whose breakout single ". . . Baby One More Time" beat Aguilera's "Genie in a Bottle" to market by about eight months).[10]

Yes, it had certainly *looked* that way, past tense, but by then Britney had unmistakably edged out all the charting blondes she'd once considered peers: Mandy Moore, Jessica Simpson, and even Christina, her true rival. Following the commercial and critical successes of her debut, Christina "dove headfirst into a Spanish-language album."[11] *Mi Reflejo*, released in 2000, was immensely successful, spending nineteen weeks at number one on *Billboard*'s Top Latin Albums list and garnering a Latin Grammy Award for Best Female Pop Vocal Album.*

In contrast, Britney kept up a breakneck pace in the mainstream. She chased her record-breaking debut with another record-breaking album the following year, 2000's *Oops! . . . I Did It Again*. The sophomore album irreversibly propelled Britney to the ranks of pop legend. Christina may have won the Grammy, but Britney clinched the pop princess title. Still, in pop, there is always room—and need—to up the ante.

Nine months before Christina's *Stripped*, Britney released her first self-titled album, *Britney*. It was a new direction, a reintroduction as well as a coming-out party for the now-adult singer's (straight) sexuality. While previous albums veered closer to rock and occasionally R&B, *Britney* adopted a distinctly *urban* radio sound, as its credits attest. Britney leaned more heavily than before on juggernaut writer-producer Rodney "Dark-child" Jerkins (whose résumé includes hits for the likes of Whitney Houston, Brandy, Jennifer Lopez, Destiny's Child, and Michael Jackson) and recruited the funky duo the Neptunes—one of whom, Pharrell Williams, would use his talents in service of many a pop career transition in the years ahead. (Britney also cowrote five out of the twelve songs on *Britney*.) The album's lead single, "I'm a Slave 4 U," written and produced by Chad Hugo and Pharrell, ushered in the new sound and feel. The music video and subsequent live performances of the song—including a memorable duet with a seven-foot albino Burmese python—encapsulated an era in

---

*Despite these successes, *Mi Reflejo* is singular among the artist's otherwise anglophone catalog, somewhat symbolic of Christina's quiet embrace of latinidad. As the singer has alleged in interviews and insinuated in song, her father, the source of her Ecuadorian roots, was abusive, complicating her relationship to her own heritage. In an interview with *Latina* magazine, Christina laments the skeptics who undermine her identity. "I don't speak the language fluently. And I'm split right down the middle, half Irish and half Ecuadorean," she said, adding, "I wouldn't be questioned [about my heritage] if I looked more stereotypically Latina. Whatever that is." America and its limited interpretation of Latinx peoples makes Christina, a blue-eyed blonde with pale skin, a hard read. And yet, also, her ability to slip out of this racial code enables an artistic freedom unavailable to Latinx and Spanish-language artists even just a shade or two darker. More recent stars like Demi Lovato and Selena Gomez—also Disney alums, also white—have similarly become unqualified stars on the pop charts.

the pop star's career that became best known for three things: oiled abs, smudged eyeliner, and 808s aplenty. Onstage at the 2001 MTV Video Music Awards, the digital drums become the soundtrack to an elaborate jungle romp. Her hair is styled to look more greasy than tousled, the gauzy green top resembles bamboo leaves, while a bejeweled—or bedazzled—butterfly crosses her hip flexors: Britney pops and locks and belly-dances among backup dancers wearing textured wigs, painted in animalian stripes. The performance was barely more skin-baring and no more risqué than appearances in years past, and yet public consensus agreed that some change had occurred, something more intense, more sexual—dangerous, even.

Britney wasn't the only pop star going urban to go wild just past the turn of the new millennium. The same year that Britney body-rolled around in the understory at the VMAs, N'Sync released *Celebrity*. This third album from the mega–boy band sensation is cynical and sexy—it also, coincidentally, ups the funk factor with production by Darkchild and the Neptunes (along with writing and producing staples Chasez and Timberlake). Also that year, Jennifer Lopez's sophomore album, *J.Lo*, yielded the charting remixes "Ain't It Funny" and "I'm Real," songs that rest on the writing and vocals of a then-unsigned young R&B artist named Ashanti. The blend is almost seamless, but once in the know you can't unhear the spectral feedback in each chorus—her voice shadows J.Lo's, which in turn mimics Ashanti's. ("It was bittersweet," Ashanti recalled in an interview years later, "because it was J.Lo, but I was so mad at [producer and Murder Inc. founder] Irv [Gotti] 'cause I was like, 'You know I wanted that record!'"). While the actual syncing would go for years without note, slipping into the vocals of a black artist wasn't without some residual controversy in the year 2001—namely on the matter of *nigga*, which arrives coyly in the third verse of "I'm Real." Luckily for Lopez, the internet wasn't then what the internet is now, and time forgives all slurs.*

Meanwhile, Pink, billed as the anti-pop star, changed course in a direction opposite her peers'. She first entered the scene with R&B swag

---

*Early in 2019 J.Lo was tapped to perform a six-minute Motown tribute for the 61st Annual Grammy Awards.

and lyrics by singer-songwriter (and later *Real Housewives of Atlanta* cast member) Kandi Burruss. But given creative control over her sophomore album, *Missundaztood*, Pink transitioned to something more rockish, the sound she'd coveted all along. Though this act of rebellion inscribed her with a common pop narrative—Janet Jackson's *Control*, etc.—Pink's sonic transformation would ultimately keep her apart from her peers as one early-millennium pop star who *left* black music to find herself. "I used to think I was a chocolate pancake," she joked on the set of *Ellen* over a decade later.

Everyone else was growing up, dipping into black aesthetics of a kind. If *Britney* and *Celebrity* added more sex with funk, *Stripped* takes the gesture all the way, declaring bodily autonomy by way of hip-hop. The summer-soaked *Can't Hold Us Down* video, with Christina in her "Lady C" hat and plastic pumps, is only one sample in the Xtina experiment. The entire *Stripped* era adopted scripts and sounds once relegated to niche "urban" markets; now heard all across America from the mouth of a blue-eyed, blond girl from the suburbs. Christina wanted out—out of all the apparatuses keeping an artist like her from letting it out. Her way out was, again, less than coincidental—blackness became shorthand for maturity, autonomy, and freedom. Across twenty tracks, *Stripped* dabbles indiscriminately with R&B, rock, and all things rap and hip-hop. Only Christina's vocal impulses, diva-istic as ever, remain from the clean-cut, mildly suggestive, self-titled album where she made her debut—the Disney kid with a big voice.

Track 1 of *Stripped* opens with a strange electronic hum, not unlike the "deep note" trademark that would accompany the THX logo at the start of '90s films. Out of that hum comes voices and static. It is a celebrity gossip reel of some kind, and with all the broadcasts in competition hardly anyone gets a word in edgewise. Music—piano, high hat, bass—abruptly ends the broadcast, and Christina's voice enters the frame. We're in the early 2000s, but the '80s echo loud and clear. She's going to tell us a story about control—her control.

Helpfully titled "Stripped Intro," the spoken-word interlude consolidated her reputation, which, in the spirit of child pop stars growing up, had begun to get scandalous as Christina approached twenty. Older than

Britney by just over a year, Christina had her own ax to grind as an artist whose adolescence took place under the watchful eye of first Disney and then her record label. In a 2000 *Rolling Stone* interview, then nineteen, she told journalist Neil Strauss, "I think my personality is fighting to come out, and that personality is fighting with the image that everyone else has of me."[12] As he had done in Britney's famous 1999 feature in the same magazine, Strauss characterized Christina as a seductress stuck in the body of a young girl: look, here she listens to explicit rap music; here, she has a crush; here, she sleeps like an infant; here, her "Gerber baby-food jar" navel is revealed by an "I love Playboy" crop top. In so many words, the article resolved the furious speculation about Christina's dating and sex life, which had preoccupied gossip rags for over a year, culminating with a derogatory mention in Eminem's "The Real Slim Shady." Strauss admitted the "tabloids have had their fun with Christina lately" and included some of Christina's thoughts on the matter ("'It's such a double standard when it comes to the boys and the girls,' she complains"), while also teasing out whatever insider info might imply salacious behavior behind the scenes. Eminem's lyrics and music video reenactment, in which twenty-nine-year-old Fred Durst and twenty-six-year-old Carson Daly debate over who was the first to be fellated by the nineteen-year-old, are "lies or half-truths (you decide)," Strauss suggested. Of the rumors, "I'll just answer it on my next record," Christina told him—she released *Stripped* two years later.

Whether the artist wanted to make music out of her reply or was choosing to make the best out of a predatory Hollywood environment was unclear, but *Stripped* rolls with the punchy perils of the modern female pop star. That double standard, where men's artistic license looms large over direct reports from women, recycled by publications like *Rolling Stone* over and over again, is fodder for the project's thinly veiled autobiographical material. The album seeks to indict the industry that wants the appearance of sexual liberation, yet won't let girls become women and grow and mature the way they want to. Solidly in line with its predecessors—ideologically, at least—*Stripped* was Christina's *Like a Virgin*, her *Control*, a foray into pop music on her own terms. She fired her manager, Steve Kurtz. She cowrote fourteen out of sixteen songs and coproduced eight. She addressed deeply personal subjects like domestic violence and emotional abuse, along with themes like sexuality, girl power, and the aforementioned double standards against girls and women. "I can't hide. I'm not a puppet. I can't just sit up there and keep doing the same kind of music. It's time for me to explore," she told MTV ahead of the release.[13]

Reviews were mixed, but Christina succeeded in her campaign to grow up in the eyes of audiences. The album sold very well—over three hundred thousand copies its first week. "The title of *Stripped* screams 'Look at my privates!' but the quieter message is 'Be true to yourself,' wrote *Rolling Stone*'s Jancee Dunn, describing *Stripped* as "almost an album for grown-ups" with "sophisticated fare" and moments where Christina "can out-Whitney Whitney."[14] "*Stripped* is all over the place," said Kun, but "proves that if Christina ever really squared off with her fellow ex-Mouseketeer, she'd kick Britney's ass. . . . The genie has left the bottle."[15] Indeed, Christina was freed, but at the cost of what? Or, whom?

In her essay "Eating the Other: Desire and Resistance," cultural critic bell hooks relates an overheard conversation as a parable. While a visiting professor at Yale, she was walking near the campus "behind a group of very blond, very white, jock type boys."

> Seemingly unaware of my presence, these young men talked about their plans to fuck as many girls from other racial/ethnic groups as they could "catch" before graduation. They "ran" it down. Black girls were high on the list, Native American girls hard to find, Asian girls (all lumped into the same category), deemed easier to entice, were considered "prime targets." Talking about this overheard conversation with my students, I found that it was commonly accepted that one "shopped" for sexual partners in the same way one "shopped" for courses at Yale, and that race and ethnicity was a serious category on which selections were based.[16]

For very blond, very white, jock-type boys, surfing through co-eds of every make and model is the expected collegiate awakening, on par with passing continental philosophy, lighting up, and consuming more alcohol than any one person should. Each woman supplies a piece of the puzzle that is their sexual maturity. They cut their teeth on white girls; they gain sexual prowess from brown and black girls de facto deemed more sexually advanced and able, no matter how many or few, if any, sexual partners they've had. They reassert their dominance with light-skinned East Asian women, and—eventually—settle down with a nice white woman to fulfill their domestic fantasy. If, indeed, eighteen- and nineteen-year-old girls were courses in a catalog, brown and black girls would surely be organic chemistry—inscrutable, formidable, and vital in the transition from boyhood to manhood.

Such fetishes seep into the whole of American culture, known and perpetuated by all, including those who do not desire women. The stereotypes only appear benevolent absent historical landmarks such as the Trail of Tears, the Chinese Exclusion Act, and *State of Missouri v. Celia, a Slave,* the 1855 case that established in law that black women by definition could not be raped and therefore can seek no recourse for abuses by men. Lest anyone should suppose that the logic rests in the past, one need only look to current rates of sexual violence against Native women (more than half have encountered it), to the serial rapes by the monstrous Oklahoma patrol officer Daniel Holtzclaw and the suppressed reports of assault within Asian American communities.[17]

For white girls growing from girls to women, the myths America tells itself about women have another effect. Though protected from the hellish matrix of racial violence, there's no denying that white women, too, are pawns to men in pursuit of sexual maturity, dominance, and pleasure. The innocence reserved for white women alone becomes the source of crisis in their adolescence. Their identity formed out of the residue of everyone else's stereotype, white women never truly grow up in the eyes of the world. A petty history of feminism might look like white women, wave by wave, reaching maturity in the eyes of the state, and given license to do grown-women things like working and roughing it alone. And as any petty history of black feminism will tell you, black women have accessed these "privileges" all along. Or, per one fabulous (fictional) black elder, "that black bitch by definition tells a white bitch who she is."[18]

In many ways more restrictive than politics, pop culture holds firm to the idea that women can only be one thing and America likes its white women chaste. While black girls are read grown before they hit puberty, white women must find creative ways to own that maturity for themselves. Much as those overheard white boys-cum-men assumed their racial desires would ultimately free them, white pop stars, native to the industry as little girls and young women, need to go "primitive" to be sexual in ways whiteness doesn't afford. They, too, need to be changed. Both impulses, whether slaked by another individual or worn on the body like a costume, inhabit colonial fantasies in a "concrete search for a real primitive paradise," says hooks.[19] "Ethnicity," in this case blackness by way of hip-hop culture, "becomes spice, seasoning that can liven up the dull dish that is mainstream white culture."[20] Where Britney dabbled, Christina devoured black styles, black genres, black sounds, in order to get grown. She had plenty enough precedent but also left a mark of her own, one emulated in the decade-plus since.

The entire *Stripped* era put black culture in motion in a departure from Christina's earlier aesthetics, even as a child performer raised on jazz and soul records. A visual timeline of red carpet appearances and magazine spreads alone tell the story. Christina arrived at the 2000 Grammy Awards in an asymmetrical slinky silver dress covered in butterflies, with green eye shadow and clear gloss and a shaggy ash-blond interpretation of The Rachel (of *Friends* fame). One year later, at the 2001 Grammys, she is bronzed in a fuchsia kaftan, her eyes heavily lined, her blond hair encased in waist-length box braids. African styles and African texture proved crucial to the evolution that took place from 2001 to 2004: a braided afro at the Blockbuster Entertainment Awards; zigzagging cornrows at the World Music Awards; red-streaked micro braids at the MTV Movie Awards; cornrows tied back into a low ponytail at the Radio & Records Convention; pastel cornrows in a side part at the MTV Video Music Awards after-party. The braids, the thick ghetto-gold jewelry, the bold lip with the bold eye—none of it was new to observers raised on TLC, Da Brat, and Missy Elliott, who knew and saw their own Da Brats and Missy Elliotts walking around their neighborhoods any given day of the week.

But on blond hair, on a white woman, the styles looked unique, if only to other white people. To everyone else, they were as inventive as the dozens of issues of *Sophisticate's Black Hair Styles and Care Guide* piled high in the waiting area of any salon.

"Can't Hold Us Down" was not the beginning but the culmination of everything a pop figure like Christina could hope to gain from her transition from white to black. The track is a go-girl anthem that anticipates the oncoming fourth wave of millennial sex-positive feminism. Lyrically, "Can't Hold Us Down" is obsessed with that famed double standard, of sexual agency restricted in women, while congratulated in men. The song implies a certain girl-power populism, with frequent calls to women worldwide. In the video, women of color form the posse that declares autonomy against a group of men of color. The palette is multicultural, and yet, as the scholars Diane Railton and Paul Watson point out, "Blackness and whiteness are clearly inscribed on and through the bodies of Aguilera and Kim." Lil' Kim, Junior M.A.F.I.A. alumna and chart-topping artist in her own right, is here reduced. The custom is common procedure by now, that any given pop single comes with a rapped feature—leaving it up to the caliber of the rapper to determine the health of the pop artist's credibility. Kim enters "Can't Hold Us Down" roughly halfway through and fades to the background after her thirty-second verse is complete. Dressed in a multicolored bikini, chunky gold and black belt with a gold chain necklace to match, Kim—per usual—looks comfortable and in her element as she raps about gendered expectations around sex, a topic she's covered many times across her career. As Christina, the facsimile, sways and gestures behind her, it's clear why Kim simply couldn't be allowed camera time outside the bounds of her brief feature. This is not collaboration; it is a cosign. Like the urban setting, the break-dancing extras, the jewelry, the "Lady C" moniker, Lil' Kim is another prop to permit Christina access into this new cultural world.

She consumes not blackness but the *idea* of black aesthetics. Christina's entry into hip-hop sound, collabs with rap artists, and approximated hood style coincides with her transition from sexually suggestive to sexually explicit. Christina found a shortcut to sexuality, like Madonna before her, like Britney and Justin alongside her, like Miley Cyrus and the other

Justin, Bieber, after. Male artists take their taste, too; they are, after all, the original minstrels. Timberlake popped, locked, gyrated, and crooned his way into sex symbolism, then donned a suit when it was time to be received seriously as an artist, songwriter, producer, and actor. Justin the Younger, too, made beats and black vernacular useful when transitioning from kid sensation to bad boy. In a 2009 interview with *Shortlist*, the white Scottish DJ, singer, and producer born Adam Richard Wiles admitted he "thought Calvin Harris sounded a bit more racially ambiguous" when choosing a stage name for his debut soul record. "I thought people might not know if I was black or not."[21]

For those of a certain generation, Miley Cyrus is the more familiar story. I remember the *Hannah Montana* years clearly. This was back when Disney was still pumping out stars, if at a reduced rate, and the Disney Channel felt like the place to be for teens, or at least teen girls. For all their elementary-school-age fans, Miley's Miley Stewart and Selena Gomez's Alex Russo, of *Wizards of Waverly Place*, were teens with teen problems that, if childish, were more true-to-life than the other side of televised adolescence—shows like *The O.C.* or *Gossip Girl*, the kind of programming the CW would become known for, where drugs, sex, and intrigue are as regular as homework.

Never too keen on chunky streaks or synthetic wigs, I wasn't much interested in Hannah Montana. But when Disney released the 2007 album *Hannah Montana 2: Meet Miley Cyrus*, collapsing the fiction of the show entirely, I was paying attention. A lot of people were. The album debuted at number one in the Billboard Top 200, stepping over Kelly Clarkson, Bon Jovi, the White Stripes, Amy Winehouse, Maroon 5, T-Pain, and Rihanna. What can you say? The girls loved Miley. (Me included.)

So rehearsed is the story about the pop star who rebels, Disney was able to replicate it without the slightest disturbance to the Hannah Montana universe. It was right there, on the starkly divided double album and the double tour that I only now realize freakishly brought to life the double-bind that was integral to Miley's fictional character. It seemed like what it was supposed to seem, a debut for a new artist called Miley. The B-sided *Meet Miley Cyrus* portion of the album is darker, moody, appropriately juvenile coming from the fourteen-year-old who cowrote all ten songs. As Miley pursued a discography apart from her alter ego—while still acting, recording, and touring as that alter ego—her musical trajectory made parabolic sense. The darkly giddy "See You Again" aged into the angst of "7 Things" on *Breakout*, her first album officially unaffiliated with Hannah Montana. She followed that with *The Time of Our Lives*, a rockish and dance-pop-y *just fine* EP mostly forgotten save the outstanding single "Party in the U.S.A.," which is inextricably fused with beer-soaked memories from my freshman year in college.

Behind the music, public perception of Miley was changing to something a little less certain than before. In April 2008, a man named Josh Holly hacked into the teen's Gmail account and circulated her private photos, including pictures of the fifteen-year-old with an exposed midriff cozied up with her boyfriend, Thomas Sturges. Though the images were leaked without her consent, Miley was implicated in the scandal, her status as an icon among children and preteens called into question. That same month, *Entertainment Tonight* broke the news of a forthcoming *Vanity Fair* feature, implying the star had posed nude for photographer Annie Leibovitz. She had not—the June 2008 issue does display Miley's exposed spine while she clutches a satin blanket to her chest. It was enough for scrutiny. "Did Miley Cyrus, with the help of a controversy-courting magazine, just deliver a blow to the Walt Disney Company's billion-dollar 'Hannah Montana' franchise?" wondered the *New York Times*.[22] One Aussie rag claimed Disney executives were "plotting to push her to the side in favour of an untainted young star" (Selena Gomez).[23] And indeed, the president of entertainment for the Disney Channel, Gary Marsh, was quoted in *Portfolio* magazine saying, "For Miley Cyrus to be a 'good girl' is now a business decision for her. Parents have invested in her a godliness. If she violates that trust, she won't get it back."[24] Miley, who initially defended the "artsy" nature of the photograph, retracted her assessment in a released statement.[25] "I took part in a photo shoot that was supposed to be 'artistic' and now, seeing the photographs and reading the story, I feel so embarrassed," it read. "I never intended for any of this to happen and I apologize to my fans who I care so deeply about." That summer, Holly leaked another batch of stolen images, selfies of the star in a swimsuit and underwear.

Just over two years later, Miley's third studio album all but screams its premise. *Can't Be Tamed*, from 2010, yearns for an unfettered relationship to the world, released while *Hannah Montana*, the teenybopper TV show, dragged itself to a final season. The title track and lead single is expectedly anthemic. In the music video, Miley assumes the role of a foreign animal in captivity, on display—*literally* a caged bird (nest and all)—with a corset, dark eyeliner, bare legs, and posse of befeathered Cirque du Soleil companions. Knowing what we know, the video now looks *very* tame, but as with responses to "I'm a Slave 4 U," the media was *then* convinced this was Miley's pivot to advanced provocateur. The lyrics are bent on exonerating Miley of the crime chasing her since that *Vanity Fair* shoot, of being "not a girl, not yet a woman" with emotions and desires. If, in the tradition kept alive by Britney and Christina and Justin, all teen stars break for bad, it looked like *this* was it. It was not it.

Next comes the part most everybody knows. It is the part of Miley's career so perfectly timed to the internet content machine, the star couldn't have chosen a better moment to become black if the black Oracle from *The Matrix* had given it her black blessing. When Miley got up on stage at the 2013 MTV Video Music Awards in Brooklyn of all places and twerked against the crotch of soulful minstrel Robin Thicke, she engineered the perfect storm that thundered across broadcast news and social media. Her career was a parabola all right; we'd just misjudged the vertex. To some it was obvious, so obvious, what she was doing, what her team was doing, what the people around her—Mike WiLL Made-It, Pharrell—were enabling. It wasn't simply rebellion. The sounds and styles known both to black neighborhoods and Top 40 radio were deemed valuable. Money was beside the point; Miley was already drowning in it as a former Disney employee—incidentally, the identitarian cause for crisis. Her pop punk leanings—à la Avril Lavigne—were too cutesy still to shock rather than shake public perception. Hip-hop culture could break Miley free of the tug-and-pull game she'd been playing with her own sovereignty since she was fifteen years old. She achieved her desired end, though her means weren't novel.

As the blonde next door, Christina could, at best, call notice to her wants, tell her baby to *come on over*, and entreat listeners to rub her the right way; as the brunette doppelgänger to an on- and offscreen pop sensation engineered by children's programming executives, Miley was destined to retain the whiff of respectability. But Xtina, the tan, dreadlocked street fighter or dark-haired pimp, can gyrate and mime a hand job; Miley the hood rat can stick out her tongue and wear leotards without pants in public. They can experiment, get dirty, shock the public, seize their womanhood and then, after the fun is over, walk away like it never happened.

"**C**hristina Aguilera has recorded a new song," MTV announced in July 2004, "but" it was "not for her upcoming album," the headline teased.[26] Christina was on break of sorts, under no apparent rush to record and release another album after a joint *Justified* x *Stripped* tour with Justin and a solo tour of her own. Christina was focused on her personal life. After the kinds of public turmoil with men that surfaced on *Stripped*, she had found love and was preparing to settle down. She was ready to embark on a new chapter, as the cliché goes.

The "new song" Christina had recorded was "Hello," released in the form of a Mercedes-Benz commercial relaunching the brand's A-class sedan. Written by Christina, "Hello" utilizes the soulful qualities of her voice, jazzy if corny to befit its purpose. Leaning against the tiny European vehicle, she looks like neither the Christina to whom we were first introduced, nor the Xtina to whom we'd never truly gotten accustomed (but loved anyway in spite of ourselves). She wears loose calf-length brown trousers and a white button down, opened to just the barest suggestion of cleavage. Her hair is blond again, short with bountiful curls. Her lips are red and her skin just sun-kissed instead of bronzed. "Having it be a reintroduction, you know, the song is called 'Hello,' so . . ." she giggles, seated on set in an interview with the German TV show *Punkt 12*. "It kind of works hand in hand, so I think we make a good team together." Understated is Christina's own reintroduction, sounded in the old-school tone of the song and the put-together visual of Christina herself. "As soon as you hear the name Mercedes . . . everyone knows of course the title and the label and think[s] class, elegance, and prestige. You know, quality."

As much as Christina's "Dirrty" ego had been a shock, her post-"Dirrty" era was no less surprising, if still a relief to critics and audiences. For two years she teased the next phase of her career in one-offs such as the Benz commercial and a series of red-carpet looks that included pin curls, white fur, red lipstick, diamonds, and blonder and blonder hair. On June 6, 2006, she released a single, "Ain't No Other Man." The video followed shortly thereafter, debuting later that month on MTV's *Total Request Live*. "Ain't No Other Man" symbolized several things: Christina's euphoric love life and marriage, comprehensive creative control of her career, and the next step toward the diva existence she'd worked for since childhood. The single crystallized a transition that was visual *and* sonic. Christina was getting "back to basics," as it were, a transition that didn't mean leaving black music and styles behind but rather sounding them out in a way that would have her treated seriously as a woman *and* an artist. She was not only grown up but mature. A woman of *quality*.

The video for "Ain't No Other Man" opens in the alley of reimagined 1920s Harlem. Christina, the credits tell us, stars as her new alter ego, Baby Jane, a fast-talking, soul-singing pinup girl. "Ain't No Other Man" is not so much concerned with historical consistency as with the feel of a faraway American past. It cuts from an underground speakeasy to a lavish French dressing room to a cozy studio apartment to the red carpet to a pool hall. The costumes and props are all a little flapper, a little Old Hollywood, a little Josephine Baker, a little *Gentlemen Prefer Blondes*, a little Chicago, a little New York, a little Los Angeles, a little "war to end all wars," and a little World War II.* The song, too, evokes the feel of a classic past without strict adherence to the sound of any particular time. It samples from the '69 funk and jazz records "The Cissy's Thang" by the Soul Seven and "Hippy, Skippy, Moon Strut" by the Moon People, which take on a big-band feel in their new context. Altogether everything looks and sounds old school, never mind which one.

Back to Basics makes its influences known immediately. Christina again begins with an intro track, a thesis statement of sorts for the direction

---

*Christina would later play up a more strictly '40s vibe in the music video for "Candyman."

of the album as a whole. She rides the border between scat singing and sing-talking of legends and tributes and rhyme and melody. No names are mentioned, but it's far from mysterious whom Christina evokes, whom she wishes to embody in her quest of getting down to basics. Later on the album she pays homage to these figures more directly with songs like "Back in the Day," which name-drops Donny Hathaway, Lena Horne, "Miss" Aretha Franklin, Minnie Riperton, Louis Armstrong, Marvin Gaye, and Billie "Lady Day" Holiday over a DJ Premier beat reminiscent of '80s rap. Another song, "Understand," riffs off the 1967 Betty Harris "Nearer to You." These and other songs, much like "Ain't No Other Man," are an amalgamation of black musical styles across the twentieth century called in to manifest a classic feeling and in turn provide an opportunity for Christina to emit "class, elegance, and prestige." From *Stripped* to *Back to Basics*, Christina swings from one interpretation of black culture (young, trendy, gritty, sexualized) to another (older, elegant, sensual, classic).

Publications were eager to scrub off any grime leftover from the *Stripped* era. The same places once titillated by Xtina's provocative antics now ran headlines such as "Dirty Girl Cleans Up" (*Rolling Stone*), "That Dirrty Girl, Cleans Up Real Nice," and "No More Teen-Pop Fluff: Aguilera Tries Being a Serious Singer" (*New York Times*). The copy paints her transition as nothing short of miraculous, even reigniting comparison with her rival who wasn't quite a rival anymore. In contrast to Britney, now struggling with health issues and public scandals, "It's her former rival, Ms. Aguilera, who has found the road of respectability." Though *Stripped* was supposed to represent the *real* Christina, it resembled a bad dream from the other side—indeed, a rebellious phase to be grown out of.

In this neat narrative, Christina's "dirrty" moment sounds accidental, the wayward antics of a young sensation given the reins a bit too early. Yet in the lead-up to *Back to Basics* as well as in the album itself, Christina expressed little if any regret for that period in her life. In interviews since, she's discussed the era as the messy, necessary evil she wouldn't trade for the world. "The great thing is that everyone, whether you loved it or hated it, had an opinion about that song, and everybody talked about it," she told journalist Lola Ogunnaike.[27] Songwriter and producer Linda Perry, who worked closely with Christina on *Stripped* and *Back to Basics*, implies intentionality. "She was going to turn people off before she turned them on, and it worked."[28] Christina told Ogunnaike ahead of the album's release, "Just like I knew I was going to be far more than that genie in a bottle, I knew I wasn't going to be that girl in chaps forever."[29]

In stride with a career that might as well have begun in some downtown Philly record shop, *Back to Basics* is the album Christina wanted to make all along. There's an air of *finally* about the project, like she traversed sixteen years' worth of frustration, rumors, and costume for just this moment. And yet, *Back to Basics* is still playacting. It is not a bad album, but her excavation of black music's ghosts fails to demonstrate its due commitment to history. "Aguilera doesn't need to reincarnate Sarah Vaughan to be a serious singer," wrote music critic Sasha Frere-Jones in his review of the album.[30] Sonically, "There are precious few audible connections to any music predating the seventies soul of Stevie Wonder."[31] And despite reliance on DJ Premier, the album also refuses to engage with black music's present or recent past. Christina left that behind in *Stripped*—like soul, funk, and R&B had died after Stevie Wonder's 1976 album *Songs in the Key of Life*. "I know that twenty years from now, she wants people to refer to her as she refers to Aretha, Nina Simone and Billie Holiday," Perry once remarked.[32] It almost goes without saying that what made Aretha Aretha, what made Nina Nina, and Billie Billie was their full-throated embodiment of a craft that went deeper than the skin.

In the years since *Back to Basics*, Christina has tried on robotnik electropop and collaborated with prolific songwriter and producer Max Martin, someone she dismissed in the past for his too-consistent pop successes with artists such as Britney and the Backstreet Boys. In between, she starred in and recorded an album for *Burlesque*, the fun and flashy 2010 film about a down-on-her-luck vocalist who finds stardom as a performer in a '30s-style burlesque club (the parallelism borders on divine): "It takes a legend . . . to make a star," the poster reads.

On 2018's *Liberation*, released after a six-year hiatus, she returns to the genre that has always fed her, R&B, with one crucial difference. Underlain with trap beats and exhibiting the production influences of Kanye, MNEK, and Anderson Paak, the album feels more honestly contemporary than anything since her self-titled debut. Black music made her, and

Christina could never truly leave black music behind and remain herself. Admiration finally, *finally*, turned into homage. Her voice remains quintessentially hers, melting with all the rhythmic ways soulful music has evolved in the past decade. The cover of *Liberation* captures her portrait, the depth of field so shallow as to leave only key facial features in focus, black and white all over. She *is* a star, giving honor and grace to black icons of old without losing herself in the process.

CHAPTER 2

The Cover Girl

Blackness, Groundbreaking

"Home!—a beautiful word that, isn't it, for an exiled wanderer?"

Something odd was going on with white people in America. November 12, 2014: Kimberly Noel Kardashian West breaks the internet. She's the announced cover girl for the winter issue of the quasi-edgy New York–based *Paper* magazine. Minimal, in standard *Paper* fashion, the cover says very little. "Break The Internet/Kim Kardashian" reads the blocky white font. Kim, center, has been shot from the back, eyes making contact from over her left shoulder, mouth slightly open as if surprised. She is nude save for three items: pearls corseted about her neck like Ndebele rings, a black sequin dress held just below her bare ass by hands encased in black satin gloves. (Another, tamer version of the cover shows Kim in profile, laughing, her dress hiked up above her chest, catching a foaming stream of uncorked champagne in a glass balanced on her protruding posterior.) The full set of photographs all depict the same scene, all by the noted French photographer and all-around art person Jean-Paul Goude. In one, Kim turns her breasts to the camera; she still holds up the dress, but the gloves have been tossed among the puddles on the floor, beside the turned-over glass and half-finished bottle of champagne. Her bright, open-mouthed smile accentuates the folly atop her head, a sleek double-knot with fanned-out ends. Kim's tan but not quite brown skin shines slick with some sort of lubricant and just barely contrasts with the terra-cotta background.

The shoot hails the work that made Goude famous. The balancing act with the champagne glass exactly replicates his 1976 *Carolina Beaumont, New York*, in which a nude black woman in an identical pose sends champagne to a glass balanced on her lower back. The photographer's '80s collaborations with artist-producer-model-icon Grace Jones, and the art that followed, exhibits a similar obsession with unusual body-made shapes and brown skin that looks painted on. That particular brand makes itself known in Goude's take on a Kardashian, with one crucial difference. She is not black, nor even *really* brown at this point in her career. The jungle fascination that makes Goude more than a bit imbricated in practices of racial surveillance and spectacle given just a cursory visual analysis—"Blacks are the premise of my work," he told *People* in 1979—seems tamer when appropriated onto Kim's tan but not-quite-brown skin.[1] Kim is on display, yes, but only because she wants to be.

In accord with the photographs, writer Amanda Fortini's afternoon with Kim begins with a tour of her physique, "a physical body where the forces of fame and wealth converge." Thick hair, full lips, large eyes, doll-sized feet and hands, "eyelashes that resemble miniature feather dusters," and "ample curves." Many stories about Kim start this way, awed first and foremost by the skin she's in. And a compartmentalized jaunt through her physical features might as well summarize her career—shorthand engineered by her and emulated by her siblings. The Kardashian empire began as a PR nightmare: a leaked sex tape featuring the least talented Norwood sibling caught with Paris Hilton's less famous friend who also happened to be the daughter of O. J. Simpson's late friend and defense attorney. Kim and her mother-slash-imminent-manager Kris Jenner spun the media circus into reality television gold and turned the stars of an E! network hit into American royalty.

To call Kim's body her only commodity would be disingenuous. More accurate to say the public's unwavering gaze on her body allows her to accumulate capital elsewhere. Fans and certain feminists will gut-check the implication that Kim's body makes her money, as if it's an insult. And I suppose in normative society it is—we tend to treasure so-called cerebral employment above the category called physical labor. And yet, are academics and accountants and programmers paid not only to think but to actively engage in the erosion of their eyesight and lower spine for many hours a day, many days a week, many months, many years? Do they not work such jobs in order to spend their checks on the ones who also work their bodies for checks: personal trainers, waitresses, strippers, athletes? Kim is not a sex worker, yet we balk at the idea that her body makes money, which ultimately reflects worse on how our culture treats sex workers than on the respectability of their work.

Certainly eking out hundreds of millions of dollars from one's God-given gifts is not so simple, even if those gifts have been tweaked, nipped, and filled out. If Kim were truly, Anglo-Saxon-y white, we probably wouldn't know her name. If Kim were unwaveringly white, her consolation prize for the gross violation of privacy—besides a multi-million-dollar settlement—would have been merely that December issue of *Playboy* and a kitten-eared page in a long line of Hollywood socialite mishaps. An Armenian American with an Armenian name and brown features, Kim's distance from whiteness, however relative, made her a person of interest, revulsion, and desire. She's leveraged this intersection her entire career, ethnic but not *too* much so, supplying the spice America so craves without tipping into the jungle. As her facial features evolved closer to the Western ideal, her hips grew wider, ass larger, and style more in common with hip-hop's video baddies. Kanye West fell in love with her and she became his muse, a literal video vixen. She wears bodysuits and two-piece couture that might better be found at Rainbow or Fashion Nova. She styles her hair in cornrows, calling herself "Bo West." She bottles perfume in headless molds of her naked body and then posts the photos of that naked body (head attached) on Instagram like a living Venus of Willendorf. All the while courting the attentions of an American public that is less amused when black women show skin.

Her younger sisters managed to up the ante in their blackified antics. Khloé Kardashian and Kylie Jenner, who might unkindly be considered the plain Janes of an admittedly very attractive clan, found favor in a full-bodied embrace of hood culture. Cornrows, do-rags, grills, bling, weave—these staples of black ingenuity throughout the decades adorn their bodies where bad bangs and empire-waist dresses once were. At times, imitation has drifted to outright forgery: in 2017, Khloé's Good American line was shown to have lifted designs from black designer Destiney Bleu after Khloé placed orders with Bleu's line the year prior; just a week later, Plugged NYC noticed the resemblance between its merchandise and apparel sold from the Kylie Shop, and posted the receipt of Kylie's order with the black-owned brand. *That same* summer, both Kylie and another sister, Kendall, released a line of faux-vintage T-shirts that superimposed their faces onto those of major musical figures, including but not limited to Tupac Shakur and Biggie Smalls, without permission from anybody's estate. "I have no idea why they feel they can exploit the deaths of 2pac and my Son Christopher to sell a t-shirt," Voletta Wallace, B.I.G.'s mother, wrote on Instagram. "This is disrespectful, disgusting, and exploitation at its worst!!!"

What fashion can't, digital and surgical intervention will, in this case transform each sister into the black girl of her dreams, a conglomerate of a regula black girl from the block who exists nowhere and everywhere. Khloé, forever thick in eyes of thin-obsessed Los Angeles, finessed her way to a sort of *thicc* cosplay, redirecting her fat and our eyes to that part of the body deemed the black's most valuable export. Her 2015 cover for *Complex* magazine plays up a boss-ass-bitch-meets-chola aesthetic—chunky gold jewelry, pouty lips, wavy wet-look hair and all—better known to girls from places a woman like her would never go. When Khloé wore her hair in chunky cornrows, trend spotters fumbled for what to call such an inventive style (*New York Post* landed on "boxer braids"). She once called herself a "Bantu babe," sporting Bantu knots before a crowd on Instagram. The post was promptly deleted, but the internet is forever.

Kylie, coming into her own among a racially diverse circle of the young and wealthy, latched on to hip-hop culture during the transition from teenager to legal adult. She appeared in music videos for PartyNextDoor, Jaden Smith, and her boyfriend, Tyga (who began dating seventeen-year-old Kylie when he was twenty-six). After Tyga, she began dating rapper Travis Scott; shortly after their relationship went public, Kylie gave birth to their child, Stormi. Across her late adolescence, she also parlayed a minor public scandal into a profitable enterprise. Her fuller and fuller lips, read-ily available to paranoid analyses through her documentarian habits on Instagram, created speculation that the teen had gotten lip injections, a cosmetic procedure that temporarily inflates that area with shots of hy-aluronic filler such as Restylane or Juvederm. Shortly after admitting to some nonsurgical assistance with her pout—covered with much fanfare on an episode of *Keeping Up with the Kardashians*, naturally—Kylie launched the line of lip products that launched her namesake cosmetics brand. A symbol of Kylie's Kardashian canny, the Kylie Cosmetics logo displays a mouth dripping in product, open to show shiny grill-covered teeth. Her followers haven't been all the way duped, however. What makeup can't, nonsurgical intervention will. Fillers are as pedestrian as blond highlights. Big lips are in—on some.

The spidery extent of this family's investment—aesthetically, never economically—in racialized features and black styles could yield an en-tire day's delight for two experts well versed in the wider Kardashian universe. They could cackle over the time Kris found herself blinged out, flashing imaginary gang signs in a circle of tall tees, or tsk-tsk-tsk over Kim's flagrance in the face of Rhymefest, her visit to Trump's desk on behalf of "prison reform."* They might spar over the fates of the next generation, a topic made urgent by the fact that Kim, Rob, Kylie, and Khloé all have black children. All this good fun would barely breach the sea of signifieds from which the West-Kardashian-Jenners sip their fill. However, they do only what fashion and beauty allow them to do. And fashion and beauty, twin titan industries that dictate so much in the lives of the femme-identified, have better mastered the art of selling black and brown women from the block. One can find blackness on offer at any

---

*On May 31, 2018, Kim visited the White House primarily to plea for clemency on be-half of Alice Marie Johnson, a sixty-three-year-old black playwright confined to federal prison since 1997, serving a lifetime sentence for a first-time nonviolent drug offense. A week later, Trump commuted Johnson's sentence. Since taking office, Trump has also pardoned Joe Arpaio, the sadistic former sheriff who tortured inmates, and Dinesh D'Souza, a far-right conspiracy theorist spared from a prison sentence for an illegal cam-paign contribution.

price level; the everyday people behind the looks left right where they can be found.

I t was a glorious rave. Pounding, driving, unsoftened sound, smoke, and mood lighting. Tiny silver and teal shorts, tight miniskirts, camo jackets, and platforms like small skyscrapers in any shade you please—red, Kelly, purple. Thigh-high socks and patches stitched precariously, or at least the illusion of such. Tiny women wearing metallic eye shadow and tiny metallic purses and big shoes and even bigger hair—dreadlocks dip-dyed pink, purple, and sidewalk-chalk blue and piled about the head in an elaborate knot. It was a glorious rave.

In 2016, Marc Jacobs attracted a small controversy when he sent his spring 2017 ready-to-wear down the runway during New York Fashion Week. The scrutiny had nothing to do with what the models, dressed as rococo ravers, wore on their bodies but rather what was on top of their heads: candy-painted dreadlocks. Jacobs said he was first inspired by the multicolored dreads of *The Matrix* codirector Lana Wachowski, who had been announced as the face of the Marc Jacobs brand's spring-summer 2016 season earlier that year. For the forthcoming show, Jacobs recruited a locs specialist, a white Etsy shopkeeper named Jena Counts, along with Anglo-Spanish stylist Guido Palau, who installed and "texturize[d]" the locs for the occasion.[2] Palau mentioned numerous influences for the looks that eventually bounced across the stage that evening, including raver culture, Boy George, and the '80s decade in general. When *New York* magazine's Kathleen Hou asked the stylist if he'd found any inspiration in Rasta culture, he responded simply, "No, no at all."[3] Jacobs, to his credit, seemed to rethink the show a year later. He told *InStyle*: "What I learned from that whole thing, what caused me to pause after it died down a little bit, was that maybe I just don't have the language for this, or maybe I've been insensitive because I operate so inside my little bubble of fashion."[4] The next year, Jacobs's models wore turbans and head wraps.

Worth so much more, Meryl Streep's Oscar-nominated performance as Miranda Priestly gets remembered for two, albeit stunning, moments.

Hustling along to a meeting with the staff of the *Vogue*-inspired fictional *Runway* magazine, Priestly sends florals to a well-deserved grave. Elsewhere in the film, she absolutely withers Anne Hathaway's Andy, the aspiring journalist fortunately unfortunate to land a job as assistant to the mother of fashion editorial, who assumes it all—*gestures vaguely to the industry*—irrelevant to her daily life.

> Oh, OK. I see, you think this has nothing to do with you. You go to your closet and you select out, oh I don't know, that lumpy blue sweater, for instance, because you're trying to tell the world that you take yourself too seriously to care about what you put on your back. But what you don't know is that that sweater is not just blue, it's not turquoise, it's not lapis, it's actually cerulean. You're also blindly unaware of the fact that in 2002, Oscar de la Renta did a collection of cerulean gowns. And then I think it was Yves St. Laurent, wasn't it, who showed cerulean military jackets? And then cerulean quickly showed up in the collections of eight different designers. Then it filtered down through the department stores and then trickled on down into some tragic "casual corner" where you, no doubt, fished it out of some clearance bin. However, that blue represents millions of dollars and countless jobs and so it's sort of comical how you think that you've made a choice that exempts you from the fashion industry when, in fact, you're wearing the sweater that was selected for you by the people in this room. From a pile of "stuff."

The moment amazes not simply because it summarily dresses down a self-important youth who scoffs at the expertise of an elder. I age further from Andy's postgrad naïveté with each passing year, yet even the nervous teenager who saw *Devil Wears Prada* for the first time could not help but feel with Priestly in this instance. The lines captivate with their movement. Streep provides a slight serpentined drag, as if the handiwork of a woman making a million micro-calculations per instant, searching and retrieving and translating each historical artifact for the benefit of someone who surely doesn't deserve it, but absolutely deserves this read. Though fashion is the subject of the matter, you might substitute each noun with any other trickling jargon as a prescient reminder that we are unwittingly bound to decisions made above us, on our behalf.

However, the monologue conveniently elides the no-less-chilling matter that those decisions made on high are, too, influenced by the people who live and move about at the bottom. "What has always irritated me about that clip is that the fashion designer who showed it in 2012 probably stole it from some kid they saw on the street who was very stylish," *The Cut*'s Stella Bugbee remarked years later.[5] Fashion "trickles up and then it trickles back down." Just as Andy's cerulean sweater represents the long-fingered reach of high fashion, pastel dreadlocks weren't the brainchild of Jacobs or Palau (or Wachowski, for that matter). Even Counts, the white woman based in Palatka, Florida, who dyed over 12,500 yards of yarn for the show and continues to sell her custom wool dreadlocks online with many five-star reviews, did not dream up or even revolutionize a product intended to imitate the look of anglicized dreadlocks, which are themselves the unwashed, matted answer to dreads palm-rolled or twisted from afro-textured hair. Black hairdressers have, of course, developed their own fiber alternatives to the years and patience required to grow glorious waist-length locs of one's own, an innovation Counts evidently decided not to consult on the journey to perfecting Dreadlocks by Jena.

While the fashion industry demands an ongoing bibliographic record of who did what which way, weeding out counterfeits, naive assistants, the working class, and anything that might disturb the sanctified lineage of designer fashion, the industry also relies on the underclasses to breathe new life into the same tired old lines, patterns, and schema. "In fashion, there is a fine, sometimes indistinguishable line separating inspiration and theft," the *New York Times*' Katherine Rosman has written.[6] Palau, who denied his work bore any connection with Afro-diasporic tradition, had sampled from black styles prior. He gave a cast of predominantly white models cornrows for Valentino's *African* spring 2016 show, immortalized by coverage in *Vogue*. Designers Maria Grazia Chiuri and Pierpaolo Piccioli without irony placed themselves in the tradition of Pablo Picasso, whose predilection for the Africa of his own imagination secured his spot in the European avant-garde.* "The message," Piccioli told *Vogue*, "is tolerance. And the beauty that comes out of cross-cultural expression."[7] Less than a year later, Palau sent another set of mostly white models down the runway wearing Bantu knots for the house's pre-fall 2016 collection. Palau told the *Huffington Post* that the style came from '90s Björk, "a continuation of last season with that very girly, punky vibe. It's kind of the same girl, but she's going to a rave now."[8]

The list of publicized gaffes in designer fashion in recent history is long, exceeded only by quieter appropriations that never make it into the press. Louis Vuitton's 2012 spring menswear collection included Maasai-inspired scarves selling at $1,000. For its spring 2015 show, DKNY gave models long, sweeping baby hairs, styled after women born with kinky hair textures who've developed practical and artistic means of smoothing down their edges. Late 2018, a Prada store in NYC was caught displaying a line of figurines and key chains closely resembling blackface minstrels. (The figurines retail for $550.) Soon thereafter, in early 2019, Gucci issued an apology for its sale of an $890 black balaclava featuring a pair of exaggerated red lips to be pulled over the wearer's face. This, not two years after Gucci plagiarized the legendary black tailor Dapper Dan in its 2018 Cruise collection and called it "a homage." But high fashion is not alone.

Cost-effective "fast fashion," cherished for the ability to turn around runway look-alikes by the start of the season, has instituted an aesthetic regime all its own, one impacted but not dictated by the Miranda Priestlys of the world. Advantaged by a heavier reliance on poor, underpaid workers (nobody looks for "Made in Italy" on an H&M tag) and freer seasonal schedules, fast-fashion retailers can bypass the runway and find the same *inspiration* at its source. Able to recall the heyday of Abercrombie & Fitch's all-American girls, I recognize their mutations while perusing the virtual racks of the teen mecca Forever 21. The models are still white, of course, white or ambiguously quote-unquote ethnic, which

---

*According to the art historian William Rubin, Picasso encouraged the rumor that he was of African descent. (Rubin quoted in Michael North, *The Dialect of Modernism: Race, Language and Twentieth-Century Literature* [New York: Oxford University Press, 1998].)

is just to say they might be a person of color or simply a white woman with an Italian last name—which is *really* to say that everyone is tan, and not orange, in a might-be-from-SoCal sort of way. In that same sort of way, everyone is in hoops, gold hoops, to be precise, with gold necklaces (plural), and gold rings (also plural) on each finger.* And not the tasteful, maybe "sixteenth-birthday present from the child-free aunt" category of gold, but the gaudy, ostentatious, got to *got to* be faux type of show-me, you-won't-miss-this-honey gold. They are available for purchase, priced above beauty-supply stores—at once cheaper and more expensive than the real thing.

The styles, as they slide from '90s to '00s revivals, nonetheless adhere to the guiding light that approximates black style. Retro-like band tees broadcasting affinity for Run D.M.C. and Biggie have been replaced by tube tops, camisoles, and crop tees in deliberately synthetic-looking fabrics like spandex and "velvet," aka polyester, with the words "Baby Girl" or "Harlem" across the chest. One top worn by a glowy blond model harks back to the jersey dress era (which here refers not to the cozy fabric but the body-hugging minidress made to resemble an athletic jersey, ideally for a team with some sort of bygone clout like the Lakers, Bulls, or Knicks). It is yellow, solid black on the sides with a figure 95 on the front. What that number signifies it's hard to tell. It is, most plausibly, a reference without a referent, an empty gesture, as these things usually are.

Lest I forget the boys, the too-cool-without-trying slimfitters who fill out menswear ads, there, too, we can spot black-boy influences where

---

*When asked about the origins of the "Carrie" necklace, which became synonymous with one of *Sex and the City*'s most poignant Carrie moments, the show's costume designer, Patricia Field, was conspicuously vague. "I have a shop in New York City, and a lot of the kids in the neighborhood wore them," she told *InStyle* in 2015 (Claire Stern, "Patricia Field Explains the Origin of the Carrie Necklace from Sex and the City"). "I thought, 'Maybe I'll show it to Sarah Jessica and she'll like the idea.' She did, and she made it happen. It became a universal, long-lasting thing." Field neglects to mention that nameplate jewelry had already been a thing—for black and brown girls living in the boroughs and 'hoods Carrie and the gang would never frequent. Says the NYC native and journalist Collier Meyerson, "Nameplates have always leapt off the chests of black and brown girls who wear them." They are thickly beautiful but also small emblems against respectability. Like hoops and neon five-inch heels, the necklace possesses the power to make whites scrunch their nose in offense. Until Carrie made it chic.

too few black boys may be found.* The translation occurs more subtly in the sense that everything within the acceptable bounds of men's fashion must present itself subtly, without comment, without the indication that men actually give a shit about what goes on their bodies. The skinny jeans seated below the waist to reveal the broad, brand-name waistband of jock-hugging briefs; basketball shorts as casual wear; jerseys as casual wear; sneakers as casual and semiprofessional wear; the stripped-down basic sneaker for nothing but being ain't shit in someone's house; the limited and expensive multisyllabic colorway collected and treasured by those called "sneakerheads"—who, like their close cousins, "hip-hop heads," grow less and less melanated by the minute as regular "streetwear" prices surge to extravagant heights.† Reddit's "Basic Bastard" wardrobe, an easy online how-to for men upgrading from free college T-shirts to something more adult, amazingly looks like the watery residue of hip-hop's take on preppy—Tyler the Creator for the less adventurous set.

Designers, executives, and shareholders stake their wealth on imitation without attribution. Profits might not even be profits if brands were financially beholden to the individuals and cultures responsible for moving fashion forward. Appropriation is a boon also to editors, stylists, photographers, bloggers, and consultants who are paid in both money and cachet to corroborate the dependency. Black people, when their exceptional brilliance and extraordinary luck permit entry to the rarefied ranks for a purpose besides wearing clothes well, must wear the albatross of "The Only One," per the title of critic Hilton Als's profile of queer black fashion dignitary André Leon Talley. "It's exhausting to be the only one with the access, the influence, to prevent the children from looking like jigaboos in the magazine—when they do appear in the magazine," he's quoted as saying. "It's lonely."[9]

---

*An August 2017 article in British *GQ* credited Harry Styles with bringing thick, ostentatious men's rings into fashion, like men of color on the street haven't decorated their hands that way for decades.

†Nightmare vision: Bella Hadid in gold hoops, gold choker, and hair like something out of *Sophisticate's Black Hair Styles and Care Guide* next to a wall of Nike sneakers. "If homeboy's coming through with these, it's quiet."

The answer to a sartorial anxiety of influence comes readily: support black. Not just businesses, but designers, hairdressers, stylists, photographers, and reporters who know a doobie wrap when they see one coming down the American Music Awards red carpet. But this call to ethics obscures what is a problem of seeing as much as a problem of spending. Miranda Priestly exactly articulates the power imbalance between consumers and tastemakers, a monologue incidentally prompted by the ability for everyone in the room to see what Andy cannot perceive. Their sight isn't better, merely better trained to pick out aesthetic differences that *matter*—to themselves and others in power. Needless to say, black aesthetic innovations don't matter until repurposed by the select group of people who do. For the fashion world to truly cite the aesthetics that make it possible would mean ripping out the very parameters of *reinvention*. It might mean doing away with reinvention as an organizing principle, for so much reinvention is not an appropriation of the past but an appropriation of the present on a blank canvas. It might mean the end of houses, the end of Fashion Week, the end of "high" and "low," the end of trend forecasts written by anyone who isn't a fifteen-year-old brown girl from Chicago's West Side, the end of "who are you wearing" answered with the name of the person who hasn't touched a hem in decades, the end of brands, the end of "hits and misses" where the "misses" will in a few years be on trend so long as the right designer can find the right young white celebrity to shill their horrible take on a "harem" pant. It might mean the end of designers. It might mean the end of fashion.

A perky red-faced woman with long blond hair invites millions of viewers to "Get glam with me!!" What follows may be spectacular for some but is rather banal to the millions of others long initiated into this once-emergent class of YouTube natives called "beauty gurus." The "cake up and creativity," as the woman calls it, begins with a layer of foundation, the very pale, very flat liquid color applied from neck to forehead with a round sponge, spread over cheeks, under eye sockets, and around the lips. She adds a layer of concealer in almost the same shade—brighter by just a tad—underneath her eyes before blotting more pale product, a powder, on the lines around her eyes, under cheekbones, in the corners of her mouth. Her face is "set." Sparse and light as the rest of her, her brows are in an instant "done": two broad arches, brown and dark to frame her face. She "primes" her eyes—each lid becomes the mini canvas for the complementary neon fire and blue masterpiece created by patting, blending, tapering, and making gradient the concentrated pigments applied by brushes of various sizes. In another instant, her upper eyelashes have darkened and grown in triplicate. Her outer eye corner is extended by a midnight-black triangle known as a "wing." She coats her lower lashes with a mascara to look as if an additional set of "falsies" had been added. Four powders—two brown, one light pink, one shimmery pink so light as to be almost white—bring back dimension to angles in her face and color back to her cheeks. Peach lipstick and gloss bring color back to her lips. Full glam is achieved.

There's little that is typical about Nikkie de Jager, better known as NikkieTutorials, who has over the past decade built a platform of over eleven million subscribed viewers through the wonderful, weird, and awful power of YouTube. She is enthusiastic but reserved, skilled yet approachable, and instructive in a way that stands apart from a medium known to attract extremes in either direction. And yet NikkieTutorials also epitomizes *on-trend-ness*, namely the script for an aspirational beauty practice. A large number of women and male femmes called gurus adhere to some approximation of these steps, adapted to individual tastes and experiments. One guru powders before foundation; another prefers brush to sponge; contour stick over bronzer. All invariably cycle through an unending list of brand-name products—one clue as to how monetized the whole thing has become.

A cut crease here, a contoured nose there, a forehead highlight here, and dramatic lashes there, beauty industry is all about a "beat face."* A

---

*Things are changing, though. Companies like Glossier and Milk Makeup have led the shift to skin-first makeup, entreating consumers to pair elaborate (and expensive) skincare with minimal product. The prime Glossier Girl leaves the house with natural, dewy, youthful skin unencumbered by layers of "cake."

beat face looks *did*, flawless, and stays in place all day or night. Contour kits and setting products and specialized tools have trickled down from expensive brands only patronized by makeup artists to a new class of prestige products purchased from the likes of Sephora down to what are now labeled "drugstore brands" found at any local Walgreens or Target. Compared to my teenage arsenal of concealer, eyeliner, and mascara, teens with means have dozens of products at their disposal to deftly conceal imperfections, draw out features, or just have a bit of fun. It used to be that makeup either worked or it didn't, the foundation matched or it didn't, mascara was the blackest or brown, brows were messy or clean. Now, even the casual makeup wearer speaks in jargon: oxidize, fall out, pigment, color correct, coverage, buildable, blendable, moisture-rich. Something called "flashback" identifies whether a product will shine white under flash photography, as if we are all one step-and-repeat away from total disaster and must prep accordingly.

Instagram is Tur[n]ing Girls into Drag Queens, exclaims the title of another video title. The upload belongs to the English makeup artist Wayne Goss, who boasts over three million subscribers to his channel. All of Goss's videos are written in caps lock, but the alarm rings genuine here. Prefacing his sermon with the note that it's all "just makeup," Goss expresses concern for beauty trends that, he claims, have taken techniques from drag queens and applied them to female faces "with the same heavy hand," creating a more "masculine tone." He contrasts that look with a more classic appearance he calls "clean beauty" that prioritizes skin. "We aren't trying to drag ourselves up," he adds. He compares the routines touted by gurus on Instagram and YouTube to the before-during-after transformation of the model, makeup artist, and former *RuPaul's Drag Race* season 7 contestant Miss Fame, who posts makeup tutorials on her own channel. "The purpose [of drag] is to transform a male into a heightened female," says Goss. "When you've already got a female face, all of the excess work needs to be softened."

Even if there were such a thing as an essentially female face, one might presume a working makeup artist would find few reasons why anyone wearing makeup—woman, man, neither, both—should conform to whatever that would be.* In the comment section, several anonymous users point the finger to NikkieTutorials, someone they claim has never met a layer of product she didn't like. She would probably agree—her video *The Power of MAKEUP!* celebrates makeup's transformative capacity as a form of self-expression. The six-minute video was uploaded a couple months after Goss's, and though he isn't mentioned, his lecture fits among the "makeup shaming," NikkieTutorials notices around her. Years later it is still her most popular video, at forty million views and counting.

That is not to throw all anxieties of influence out the window, but Goss, misled by the woefully contemporary division between man and woman, misses what might be properly called problematic about the transfer from mainstream drag to mainstream beauty. Much as popular makeup techniques borrow from drag, capital rarely flows to queer pioneers. Brands seldom call upon them to be the face of products, even as these products exist to imitate their looks. "Do I feel the drag community has been given the credit it deserves for highlight, contour[ing], cut creases? No I don't," Vivacious, the veteran New York queen from Jamaica, told *Elle* in 2018.[10] "Why do I say that? When was the last time you saw a drag queen in a commercial for L'Oréal, CoverGirl, anyone? We're not there."[11] Whiteness, per usual, compounds the erasure. The best-paid gurus are conspicuously whiter and lighter than the very black, very brown, working-class-if-lucky queens and queers who constitute the known auteurs of the urban dancehall scenes made visible to the public by works such as the 1990 documentary *Paris Is Burning* and the FX drama *Pose.* As so much vernacular from these scenes—as well as the club, the neighborhood, the playground, the poetry reading, the diner—is rapidly consumed by the mainstream, so, too, is the art of the in-fact culturally

---

*Drag as a diverse whole enacts artistic feats above and beyond the narrow interest of passing. Even Miss Fame, the rod with which Goss hammers sense into beatface women, appears more interested in unfolding the terms of what may be considered androgyny in her body of work. Visit Chicago's esteemed Berlin nightclub for a show or for any other reason at all and you'll find not a segregated cast of gender look-alikes but an intermingled bunch who interpret whatever gender however they imagine. I'm sure anyone who accuses the bearded queen Lucy Stoole of mimicking anybody's anything, let alone something so pedestrian as a Maybelline ad, would elicit only laughter.

capacious LGBT communities restaged to befit the normative (white) marketplace. Even the first CoverBoy, a white, openly gay man named James Charles, saw fit to joke about the possibility of contracting Ebola during a visit to South Africa and CoverGirl, still breathless from its progressive feat, saw fit to keep him.*

Like its bosom buddy, fashion, the beauty industry loves to source inspiration from the social bottom and hide the dark, queer hands responsible. While American beauty eternally reaches for so-called Eurocentric standards, that refrain often misses the industry's penchant for change. Ever since beauty acquired economy, dollars, and commercial heft, the standard has zigged and zagged to suit the whims of art, of fashion, of politics. Tans are in until they're out; first it's about the eyes and then it's about the lips; cherub faces take center stage one moment, next it's an angular structure fine enough to slice bread. People who grew up ostracized for their hairiness now smirk at the ones who draw in a set of thick brows. (These changes, of course, occur within the small field that presumes white people do everything better, even if it requires sun damage or surgery to get there.)

Yet the rise and fall of what looks good and what looks bad instructs us that change not only happens, but is sought, thirstily, by anyone who may be touched by this enterprise, which is everyone. Beauty wants cake, but will never be satisfied, only full. And so it continues the chase and will to do whatever it takes to make white people as glam as the ones who wrote the book on it. It will never happen. Beauty must settle for ghosts instead.

---

*In 2017, L'Oréal fired the black trans model Munroe Bergdorf for speaking out against racism after a white supremacist, James A. Fields Jr., drove a vehicle through a group of antiracism protesters in Charlottesville, injuring over a dozen and killing Heather Heyer.

PART II

Art and Language

CHAPTER 3

The Artist

A Dead Boy Made Art

The negroes seemed to have been killed, as the band plays in circus parades, at the street intersections, where the example would be most effective.

N kechi Amare Diallo was born November 12, 1977, sans epidural, midwife, or medical assistance in a teepee located on twenty-three acres of unspoiled land near the Montana-Idaho border on Montana's side. Under the reign of her fundamentalist parents, Diallo lived a life shaped by discipline, labor, and abuse. Mostly sheltered from the outside world—its music, its culture, its amusements—young Diallo escaped into art of her own making. As a child, she starred in her own playacting exercises, imagining herself born of another tribe, another family worlds away from the one she'd been given. She made and sold a variety of craft goods that sprouted from her mind—rag dolls, greeting cards, sucker candies, and jam, achieving near financial independence by the age of nine. Pouring the contents of *National Geographic* into her head along with whatever histories she could access from the local library, Diallo developed a more guided artistic sensibility as she matured, imbuing her work with cultural and political significance. She experimented with mixed-media collage to depict Rwandan refugees, illustrated a children's book on black hair, and accumulated art prize ribbons at the county fair.

Diallo drew, crafted, and collaged her way out of Montana, into college, into spaces and competitions and prizes much more prestigious than the Lincoln County Fair. Her Rwanda collage traveled to the United Nations headquarters, where it hung on display for a full year before being donated to Tougaloo College, a historically black liberal arts school in Mississippi. Across her college career, Diallo made a name for herself as an expert of black scenes on canvas and an expert of black history and politics in person. Like many artists, the commitments visible in her work blended seamlessly with her commitments elsewhere. And as her art grew more sophisticated, so, too, did her pursuit of social justice. Above a number of struggles that continued to plague her adult life—abuse rarely enters a person's life just once—Diallo lengthened her résumé, leading Africana studies curricula and afterschool programs for black youth. She received an MFA from her dream school, Howard University. She organized protest marches as a faculty member at Eastern Washington University. She was nominated to serve as president of the NAACP Spokane chapter.

On June 10, 2015, Diallo agreed to meet with Jeff Humphrey, a reporter with the local television station KXLY, to have what she thought would be a discussion of recent hate mail allegedly sent to both Eastern Washington University and the local NAACP. After several televised minutes of back-and-forth during which only half of the exchange showed interest in the topic of racially motivated harassment, Humphrey asked Diallo a simple question: "Are you African American?" Diallo declined to answer. The next day, an Idaho daily published a crude exposé on Diallo, née Rachel Dolezal, and photos of her younger years went public, helpfully supplied by Diallo's parents. "The images show a younger, pale, blond-haired, blue-eyed Dolezal who looks much different than the woman with caramel-colored skin now leading the Spokane NAACP and helping review claims of police misconduct in that city," the article reported. "Rachel is very good at using her artistic skills to transform herself," said her mother, Ruthanne.[1]

All hell broke loose.

When it comes to the matter of the woman formerly known as Rachel Dolezal, appearance is an easy place to start. In a definitive interview with Dolezal in 2017, author Ijeoma Oluo captures her appearance in a word: "white."[2] Dolezal does look white. She looks like a white woman who fell so in love with black cultures, she decided to borrow some elements for herself—which about sums up the life and times of the Dolezal enigma. In her 2017 memoir *In Full Color*, the artist traces the infatuation and kinship with black aesthetics that began at a young age, starting with her first self-portraits.* Four-year-old Dolezal drew herself with dark skin and black curly hair. Later, as the parentified sibling to the black children adopted by her negligent parents, she learned about black hair and skin care, knowledge she later actualized on her own body as an adult via "African" prints, micros and box braids, and a deep tan.

Visually, Dolezal makes an open and shut case. She looks no less white than Bo Derek, Khloé Kardashian, or Christina "Lady C" Aguilera. Yet, still, the woman became a spectacle, filling up news media and the talk-show circuit like nobody had anything better to do. It was less maddening than utterly, utterly fatiguing. As much as Dolezal might wake up every day of her life crawling through the thick smog of regret for her decision to meet Jeff Humphrey in good faith, black people regret it more. The performance of outing Dolezal had nothing to do with racial justice and everything to do with white-on-white crime.

While her appearance exhibits a white woman mated with black aesthetics, her work taps into another, parallel tradition: an artistic tradition. Since those first crude portraits as a child, her art has been almost exclusively fascinated with black subjects. (Dolezal "actually tried painting white people a couple times," she claims in her memoir, "but it never looked or felt right to me. I had difficulty seeing highlights and reflections on pale skin.")[3] Dolezal's psyche is not so particular. Her impulse to inhabit blackness—in life and in art—is rather a symptom of how rotely black aesthetics are appropriated onto a white canvas.

The art world, according to itself, does not have a race problem. The art world does not *allow itself* to have a race problem. Were any one entity within the network of museums, galleries, shows, curators, schools, artists, press, and millions upon hundreds of millions of dollars that make up

---

*The title of the memoir veers dangerously close to the much-loved black sketch comedy *In Living Color*.

capital *A* Art to allow for race as a topic of debate, the whole enterprise might collapse into so much dust. For the art world to admit it has a race problem, it would have to account for its centuries-long history in which peoples of color have been regularly pushed from the frame of what constitutes artistic enterprise; meanwhile, their creations have long inspired European and white American artists who deviate from the norm. For the art world to admit it has a race problem, it would have to consider how that history stretches into the present, where black aesthetics prove innovative, so long as they are not attached to black artists. For the art world to admit it has a race problem, it will have to admit the art world has an art problem.

Since 1932, the exalted Whitney Museum of American Art in Manhattan has hosted exhibitions boasting whom it considers the most cutting-edge artists on offer. The Whitney Biennial, as it's now called, at the apex of everything the art world loves about itself, makes a reliable "crib sheet for the market trends of contemporary art in the United States," as the professor and poet Eunsong Kim and the artist Maya Isabella Mackrandilal put it in the *New Inquiry*. The Biennial is a shortcut to the heart of the art world and therefore to the art world's race problem.[4] Made especially accessible to those from the outside, the Biennial is one of the few occasions to make broad, sweeping, but fairly accurate observations about art, period. After all, if the exhibition claims to be the best and most contemporary of contemporary American work on offer, it begins to look pretty suspect if that yield suffers the same fallacies in 1955 as in 2019. (That is, unless one were to suggest that America is the same America in 2019 as in 1955—which might not be so untrue.)

And every two years, with each passing Biennial, the event looks more suspicious as critics notice the way the Whitney speaks out of both sides of its mouth. For example, 2014 promised a show that would "suggest the profoundly diverse and hybrid cultural identity of America today."[5] What its curators, Stuart Comer, Anthony Elms, and Michelle Grabner— all white—failed to mention was the scarcity of artists of color with work on display, a trait shared with almost all other Biennials prior (exception: the panned 1992 show, in which white male artists were the minority). The statement sounds nice but signifies little. "The 2014 Whitney

Biennial is the whitest Biennial since 1993," Kim and Mackrandilal helpfully translate. "Taking a cue from the corporate whitewashing of network television, high art embraces white supremacy under the rhetoric of multicultural necessity and diversity."[6]

The 2014 exhibition showed its ass in an array of glitches that went beyond clumsy copy. There's the portrait of Barack Obama by photographer Dawoud Bey, displayed conspicuously on the fourth floor next to a lengthy note by Grabner. A painter and professor, in her statement Grabner identifies herself as a pedagogue in her curatorial practice as well, who aims "to create a democratic survey" and "curriculum" for artists and viewers. Adjacent to the statement, awkwardly situated above a fire alarm, the Obama portrait takes on an instructive quality. *I dare you*, provokes the juxtaposition, *I double dog dare you to find issue here. Under his eye.* If it seems unfair to delegate the work of post-racial sentiment to this image, this president, this Biennial was only working with some permissible mythology engendered by the administration from within. If America, a country enslavement founded, can elect a black man to its highest seat of power, surely no racial wound is too great to be healed.

Such faith is required to justify the inclusion of *Donelle Woolford*, whose paintings were located on that same fourth floor. *Donelle Woolford* is not the name of an artist, nor even of a real person, but the comic avatar of artist Joe Scanlan. Scanlan, also a professor of visual arts at Princeton, is a white man. *Donelle Woolford* is a black woman—sort of. She is a deceit. Her black womanhood relies on how much credence one lends to a name that denotes a concept, though I imagine sometimes she appears quite autonomous.

About twenty years ago, *Donelle Woolford* appeared to Scanlan in his studio amid his collages. "I liked them but they seemed like they would be more interesting if someone else made them, someone who could better exploit their historical and cultural references," Scanlan said in an interview with *BOMB* magazine.[7] "So I studied the collages for a while and let them tell me who their author should be."[8] The collages, like the muses, sent Scanlan Woolford. Her name was "appropriated," in his own words, "from a professional football player I admired" (a former Chicago Bears cornerback, Donnelle—two *n*'s—Woolford).

The story of *Donelle* varies: She was born in 1954 Detroit, one of three children born to a housewife mother and union pipefitter father. She was born in 1977 Detroit to middle-class parents—a lawyer father, her mother working as a healer. She was born in 1980 Detroit to middle-class parents—a lawyer father, a healer mother. The 2014 Biennial program indicates *Donelle* was "born 1977 in Conyers, GA," and she is listed like any other artist in the exhibition, sans mention of Scanlan. Included this way, *Donelle* was one of nine black artists out of 103 artists in total, or 11 percent of the black artists chosen for the Biennial. "Joe was the very first artist I asked to visit when I started on my studio-visit process for the W.B.," Grabner told *Observer* in advance of the show. "I invited both Joe and Donelle. Joe turned my invitation down, but Donelle agreed to participate."[9]

Donelle showed two paintings at the Biennial, *Joke Painting (detumescence)* and *Detumescence*, both 2013. Both riff off a series of monochromatic joke paintings by the well-known American artist Richard Prince. With ink, paper glue, and gesso, *Donelle* places "her" jokes on a linen canvas. *Joke Painting (detumescence)* reads,

> Richard is undressing in his apartment and spies a young woman doing the same across the way. He extends his cock over to her window sill and calls out, Hey babe wanna come over? She thinks for a moment and says, Sure, I'd love to. But how will I get back?

The joke is funny, crude, and phallocentric—a dick joke. The star of the scene, besides the proffered penis, extends the phallus further when we consider the common nickname for Richard. The foremost Dick is the very Prince whose work provides an additional underlying canvas for *Donelle*'s painting. But the Dick as in Richard must also be Pryor, whose comedy precedes Donelle in formative ways. And in collaboration with the Biennial, Scanlan took *Donelle* on tour to reenact Pryor in a forty-minute performance called *Dick's Last Stand*. The performance doubles as a séance: *Donelle* reanimates the dead man in a routine imagined to have been excised from history in what would have been the final episode of NBC's 1977 variety hour *The Richard Pryor Show*.

Dick's Last Stand combined the spiritual and embodied aspects of the *Donelle* project, concurrently if not in this case side by side. It wasn't the first time. By then Scanlan had accumulated working relationships with Namik Minter, Abigail Ramsey, and Jennifer Kidwell, three actors—all black women—who'd performed the role of *Donelle* at art shows and in performance pieces. (Namik Minter, a former student of Scanlan's at Yale and the first human Donelle, withdrew from the project.) Scanlan considers *Donelle* a "shared commitment" between himself and the actors, like an "ensemble," an account Kidwell reaffirms. Kidwell said she was initially turned off by the project but that *Donelle* "then became a personal challenge," she told the *Los Angeles Times*' Carolina A. Miranda during the Biennial. A Columbia University graduate with degrees in English and comparative literature, Kidwell in her work is interested in ambivalence, an agenda she brings to bear in acting and direction. Her Donelle is meek and awkward and Kidwell is "not interested in her being a fool." It was her idea to reenact Pryor through *Donelle*. The suggestion presumably could have been vetoed by Scanlan, but its actualization indicates an influence beyond the "merely" performative. "It originated with Joe, but this is now a collaboration."[10] Kidwell is no dummy.

True to Kidwell's thesis, *Donelle* places *everyone else* in the hot seat. As a white man roaming the art world with the access of white manhood and theatrics of black womanhood, Scanlan cannot be permitted to escape censure. Yet, critiques of Scanlan that override the fact of Ramsey and Kidwell risk replicating his alleged erasure, supposing these women to be at the will of one white artist, rather than artists themselves. The assumption that these women know not or care not is too reductive (and reeks of misogynoir).* Kidwell told Miranda, "People have said, 'No, you are not a collaborator!' And I'm like, 'How are you telling me that I'm not doing what I'm saying I'm doing?'"[11] That special blend of gendered racism rings familiar.

The problem is and isn't *Donelle*. The very subject of *Donelle* swallows a conversation to be had between and about people. "Our participation

---

*Coined by the scholars Moya Bailey and Trudy, "misogynoir" refers to forces of anti-black racism and misogyny that together uniquely affect the lives of black women.

could complicate what many consider a clear example of exploitation," Kidwell wrote in an essay published post-Whitney.[12] "But so far it hasn't, because Abigail and I have largely been left out of the discussion, as if *we*, like Donelle, do not exist."[13] The problem is and isn't *Donelle* because *Donelle* does not exist. *Donelle* cannot talk back except through the mind and mind and body of her keepers. The problem is not in presentation—even if she were a walking, talking relic of minstrels past, because the problem of minstrelsy isn't the shoe polish. The problem of minstrelsy is desire.

I go back to the character's genesis, a beginning that must be much less divine than Scanlan describes. It was just Scanlan then. Scanlan and his collages, which suddenly seemed less humdrum if not the product of his white imagination. His impulse brings him to black womanhood. He breathes black womanhood to life. He seeks black womanhood as a break from the usual; ironic, then, that his gesture replicates so many artistic gestures before and alongside his time. He's defended his impulse in these terms, pointing to William Faulkner and Flannery O'Connor, as if those authors didn't have their own white imaginations to contend with. Scanlan and Kidwell, so preoccupied with *Donelle*'s rightful existence as a fictional character, don't contemplate the preexistent fictions needed for her to emerge in the first place. Out of all the identities in the world, Scanlan chose a black woman, a person who, if real, would be as discounted by the world as he himself is overvalued.* Head, shoulders, knees, and toes above artists who happen to *be* black women, who struggle for a fraction of recognition from sentinels of the art world who look like him, Scanlan crouched down and plucked from them what he sees as their only worthwhile feature. Not their history, not their culture, not their community, but an identitarian claim. Scanlan played identity politics and won.

August 9, 2014: police officer Darren Wilson kills teenage Michael Brown Jr. in Ferguson, Missouri. November 24, 2014: a grand jury decides not to indict Wilson, decides not only was the teen's death *not* a crime but also that it was not worth the time to consider whether or not

---

* *If Donelle can make it into the Whitney, what's stopping y'all?*

it was a crime. Two weeks later, the St. Louis County prosecutor's office releases the federal autopsy report on Michael Brown's forever-teenage body. March 13, 2015: the prestige poet Kenneth Goldsmith premieres a new work entitled "The Body of Michael Brown." It is a "remix" of the aforementioned autopsy report, "altered," in Goldsmith's words, "for poetic effect." A medical account of the dead made "less didactic and more literary." A dead boy turned into art.

An advocate for conceptual artistic practices, Goldsmith embraces what he calls "uncreative writing." The practice is a knowing inverse to the commonly understood mission of creative authorship—to make new, to go forth with never-before-seen ideas, stories, characters, and style. But as any linguist or literary agent or casual moviegoer can tell, few if any of the ideas that come to us are original in the sense of only belonging to us. The sociologist Erving Goffman called it "embedding," the tendency for speakers to knowingly and unknowingly blend bits of others' talk into their own. Everywhere we go, every conversation we have, every screen, text, and image we see is an opportunity for parts of the outside world to intrude and influence our inner thoughts, and in turn the thoughts we send back out. Rather than fear the due process of language, Goldsmith proposes a supposedly revolutionary approach to writing by repurposing the insurmountable text already in existence. "With an unprecedented amount of available text, our problem is not needing to write more of it," he writes in the introduction to a manifesto of sorts. "Instead, we must learn to negotiate the vast quantity that exists."[14]

Appropriation, copying, sampling, even plagiarism—Goldsmith doesn't fear the kinds of words typically attributed to his kind of work. On the contrary, he and other conceptual poets like him understand appropriation as the economical and perhaps only means to say something relevant about the world around us in the digital age. Other art forms, like music, have long been hip to the game when it comes to recycling riffs, chords, and vocals for newly meaningful purposes, Goldsmith points out. Literature is late. In Goldsmith's own poetry an uncreative practice means, for example, utilizing every word of a single, banal issue of the *New York Times* for the eight-hundred-plus-page collection called *Day*. "It's a great book," he told the *New Yorker*, "and I didn't write any of it."[15] He also makes ritual the not-so-routine, such as in 2013's *Seven American Deaths and Disasters*, which replays events like the Kennedy assassinations and the attacks of September 11, 2001, as they occurred live, segmented by broadcast regularities like pop music and advertisements.

Both the routine and exemplary came together at Interrupt 3, a conference on language and art held in spring of 2015 at Brown University, where Goldsmith performed the poem "The Body of Michael Brown" for the first and—as he decided afterward—final time. I was not there. When Goldsmith took the stage I was a time zone away and, as Twitter tells me, musing on velour tracksuits while recovering from a fifteen-mile run. And so, much as Goldsmith witnesses events through the words of reports on events he was not immediate to, I must also rely on mediated testimony to reimagine this particular one-time-only performance of a dead boy turned into art.

"His reading was unemotional and relatively even and his feet moved rhythmically the entire time," said artist Faith Holland.[16] Goldsmith reportedly read the autopsy report for half an hour, though not until the end did Holland realize that the report had been reordered and in some places altered by Goldsmith. The "obscure medical terms," for example, had been "translated into plain English," Goldsmith explained in a Facebook post days later. The poem's last line, "The remaining male genitalia system is unremarkable," had been selected from elsewhere in the report. After the reading, the session continued with a planned panel discussion on the performance that had just taken place. The audience "mostly offered mild criticism but repeatedly thanked Goldsmith for 'bringing up this discussion,'" said Holland. "There was one woman who made an impassioned comment about how this was a 'spectacle' and it needed to be made meaningful in order to justify happening. She too thanked Goldsmith. The audience applauded." Panelist Ian Hatcher expressed discomfort moving forward and the session ended shortly thereafter, ahead of schedule.

As I am neither witness to the reading nor the writing nor the report nor the reason the report need exist, it is difficult to decide exactly where the violation begins. Was it sometime over the days, weeks, perhaps, months Goldsmith spent poring over page after page of sterile documentation, self-selecting the turns of phrase that would transform into literature Brown's butchered anatomy? Was it when Goldsmith "translated," as he says, the medical terms that would otherwise trip up his tongue and distance listeners—was it when he chose not to consider that maybe no death ought to be made more palatable and certainly not this one? Was it the moment—for sanity's sake I must believe in such a moment—when Goldsmith put his hysterical transcription on pause, considered maybe, *No, maybe, This is wrong.* Maybe, *This isn't mine,* maybe *This is no more found and free for manipulation than a lynching postcard found half buried in some rocks beside Myrtle Beach.* Maybe, *This here has already been so distorted that for me to intervene in this way would be less a disruption than an amplification of the already many repeated, uncreative scripts applied to a teenager thirty-five years my junior and counting.* Was it in his decision to push past all doubt and flaunt his artistic achievement at an academic institution, in this case Brown University, which required the enslavement of black people to endow itself as an institute of higher learning? Was it when his panelists allowed him to continue, when the audience allowed him to continue, when the whole event didn't stop right then and there, so full of shame that a black boy barely cold in the ground had become the means to awe and wonder at white craftsmanship? Was it when whatever intern handed or stamped and mailed the five-hundred-dollar honorarium—was it when he cashed it, or when it cleared without question of where it would go (Goldsmith donated the money to Hands Up United)? Was it when Goldsmith's shame stalled Brown University from releasing the video recording of his performance, or is it some small reparative justice that we may never witness his performance with our own senses?

Literature, though credited with propelling America's most progressive movements, often conceals the nation's most enmeshed prejudices. From Harriet Beecher Stowe to e. e. cummings—who repurposed minstrel patter to sound avant-garde—to Harper Lee, white writers across the past three centuries have played fast and loose with racial aesthetics, have been canonized in reading lists that form the basis of public school curricula without attention to their use and misuse of black figures. Even writers who remove black people from their stories are infected by a racially coded language that lazily evokes blackness for fear, deviance, and dread, while whiteness is reserved for the hopeful, lovely, and pure-hearted. As Toni Morrison explains in her 1993 study *Playing in the Dark*, black people haunt American literature like unwieldy specters in the canthus of the white imagination. Literature ingests life and informs it, animating notions while offering creative language to articulate these notions past the page. Darren Wilson, a police officer tasked with de-escalating conflict in human interactions, dreamed up a monster to justify murder. "The only way I can describe it," Wilson said in testimony, "it looks like a demon, that's how angry he looked." Wilson is responsible for his actions, but he inherits his judgment from a lifelong exposure to text, sounds, and images that conjoin blackness and evil. White writers ignore this precedent at a peril that's not their own.

The potential of Goldsmith's uncreative practice, which here chose to reinscribe the qualities of a corpse on a person who'd already been determined unworthy of life, can only be revolutionary if we do not take as the status quo the ritual and regular appropriation of black aesthetics for white authorship and audiences. When layered over a history of colonialism and power, uncreative writing looks more like the default method practiced by artists and writers (Picasso, cummings, Scanlan, and others) since the West began formally recognizing the creative arts. An anonymous group called the Mongrel Coalition Against Gringpo—"gringpo" as in gringo poetry—even uses the term "colonial aesthetics" to denote conceptual art and poetry. I struggle to find what else to call a method predicated on theft without citation, theft without remorse, theft without ethics, without the barest acknowledgment of race and gender and therefore history.

Goldsmith never apologized for his poem. He enjoyed a scholar's retreat, a series of readings and workshops throughout Europe, far from the very, very *un*-cosmopolitan American race question. Contrary to the hand-wringing, Goldsmith was not run out of poetry by a zealous crowd with pitchforks in hand. He's published books with distinguished houses, he holds a faculty position at an Ivy League university, he's been reverently featured by the *Guardian* and *New Yorker*, though in the interview with the latter, Goldsmith, the controversy still fresh, mused that maybe literature wasn't the proper place for him after all. "Sometimes I think I might be headed back to the art world," he says to Alec Wilkinson. "They still seem to like me there."[17]

Any year might be considered the follow-up to a fraught period in black American history, but 2017 felt especially raw, all things considered. The jubilee occasioned by America's first black president had since disintegrated with each publicized police murder of black children, women, and men. The year 2016 was very black, so we thought, punctuated by very black moments across mass culture—from Rihanna's *Anti* and Kanye West's "Ultralight Beam" to Beyoncé's *Lemonade* to Issa Rae's *Insecure* and Donald Glover's *Atlanta* to Barry Jenkins and Tarell Alvin McCraney's *Moonlight*. The election of one megalomaniac racist and a Congress full of co-conspirators brought the country swiftly to its senses. American politics had gone to shit (now was not the time to remind everyone how shitty American politics has always been), and if electors couldn't save us, surely the arts could. We needed art "Now More Than Ever," the op-eds hailed.

Enter the 2017 Whitney Biennial. Though over a year in the making, curators Christopher Y. Lew and Mia Locks accurately predicted their position at the precipice of what feels like a *moment* in American history, and by extension, the arts. On the exhibition website, the proclaimed "longest-running survey of American art" knows that it "arrives at a time rife with racial tensions, economic inequities, and polarizing politics"—as if any other time in American history would be on the contrary. The thematic ties between artists are described as "the formation of self and the individual's place in a turbulent society" and artists' ability to "challenge us to consider how these affect our sense of self and community." Though loose and vague in the way prestigious (albeit interesting) colloquia often are, the mystery is part of the Biennial's allure—it's an art show, after all. One must feel the times, not be told about it. That is the art of curatorial practice itself, putting the most contemporary of contemporary artists together to see what themes shake out.

After the show opened, violence soon emerged as one of those undersold themes. An installation markedly titled *Real Violence* provided viewers with virtual-reality gear for them to bear witness to a seemingly random act of assault committed by an avatar of the artist Jordan Wolfson. A white man in a gray T-shirt takes a baseball bat to the head of another white man in a red hoodie and stomps his face in with blood spraying everywhere while you, the viewer, lie prone and listen to Hebrew prayer. The piece, barred to anyone under the age of seventeen, was controversial to be sure. Some understood the harrowing experience as necessary to traverse in order to ponder a disquieting subject like violence. Many others thought the experience made violence safe and trivial.

Worse, the piece seemed to ignore the real world of violence swirling around outside the museum. It was not insignificant that Wolfson's digitized figures were white, nor was it the first time his art featured a white body beat up and brutalized. Just a year earlier Wolfson debuted *Colored sculpture*, a piece in which a life-size blue-eyed, red-haired puppet wrapped in chains is jerked about and repeatedly dropped to the floor to the soundtrack of "When a Man Loves a Woman" sung by black soul artist Percy Sledge. The artist Ajay Kurian wrote in a review, in "a moment where white victimhood is thought to be as pressing an issue as the institutionalized murder of black people in America," a display that expects audiences to once again extend endless sympathy to a chained white body was irresponsible.[18] Wolfson's *Real Violence* VR spectacle gives the visual an upgrade, leaving race unexamined once again. *Real Violence* makes white men the default victims, an unwitting reproduction of the alt-right battle cry that white masculinity is under assault. "Violence is real for many of us, not an abstraction," said *Hyperallergic* founder Hrag Vartanian in response to the piece.[19]

Sensational as *Real Violence* was, the 2017 Biennial is ultimately remembered for a more flagrant dismissal of violence and black pain. *Real Violence* was soon overshadowed by a painting on the fifth floor by a white artist, Dana Schutz, entitled *Open Casket*. Schutz re-created a 1955 photograph of Emmett Till's dead body in his casket with oils and thick, broad strokes. Within days the piece garnered criticism, most notably by artist and writer Hannah Black, who penned an open letter addressed to the Biennial curators and staff. "I am writing to ask you to remove Dana Schutz's painting 'Open Casket' and with the urgent recommendation that the painting be destroyed and not entered into any market or museum," the letter begins. The letter continues for five more paragraphs and over seven hundred words, with co-signatory support from twenty-seven individuals, including curators, activists, fellow artists, and scholars. But in the weeks that followed, that one opening sentence would become the singular impression of Black's letter. The question of who ought to profit from anti-black violence was lost to a debate about free speech, the ethics of the matter gone with the wind.

I t was the usual hot Mississippi August in 1955 when young Emmett Till went to a local grocery store and bought himself a pack of gum. Days later Roy Bryant and J. W. Milam, two white men, kidnapped and murdered Till, crushing and contorting his features beyond recognition. Bryant's wife, twenty-one-year-old Carolyn Bryant, who worked at the store, claimed Till had grabbed her and made lewd comments, testimony she repeated to a courtroom when her husband and brother-in-law were, remarkably, brought to trial. "I was just scared to death," she said, words that would worm themselves into the mouth of a twenty-eight-year-old cop almost six decades later. Five decades later, Carolyn allegedly admitted to having told the lie that every black person in America been knew.* White people in 1955 or 2014 or 2019 do not need actual threats or slights to commit acts of violence—imagination is enough. The ghost in the corner.

Gruesome death often calls for a closed casket. I've heard people say funerals are not for the dead but for the living, but that's not quite true. For black folks, funerals are a celebration of life, a very special someone's life, to propel the dead person to the great beyond and remember them as they moved about Earth, body and spirit. Mamie Till-Mobley, her son's face so disfigured he could only be identified by the initials inscribed on a silver ring, left the casket open. That alone was a hard-won task, emotionally to

---

*Timothy Tyson's 2017 book, *The Blood of Emmett Till*, claims that Carolyn Bryant Donham recanted the story of her encounter with Till in a 2008 interview. Donham's daughter-in-law disputes this ("Emmett Till Murder: Did Carolyn Bryant Donham Recant? The Quote Wasn't Recorded," *Chicago Sun-Times*, August 22, 2018). As far as anyone knows, Donham is still alive, but her whereabouts are being kept secret out of concern for her safety.

be sure, but also literally, as a doing to be done. Mississippi police determined that the body was *too decomposed* to warrant any action besides an immediate burial. Till-Mobley wanted the body in Chicago. The body was only released to her on the condition that the coffin would remain closed. Till-Mobley left the casket open, permitted photographs, invited mainstream (white) press to bear witness. But the white press wasn't interested. A young Negro weekly was. *Jet* took up the story and published the images of Till in his casket, a decision that left the course of its publication forever changed. *Jet* was willing above others to force America to witness the gruesomeness it had wrought.

In this next millennium, routine white violence is recorded, televised, and circulated via every medium imaginable. The days and weeks that follow these deaths caught on film and social media are like a stroll down some sort of macabre moving portrait gallery. In this way, our present day is quite unlike 1955. Mamie Till-Mobley, thrust into activism, took control over her son's image in death, plain evidence of what America does to black children. Today, footage of a black person's final moments becomes a means to wade in those final moments, hover over them, rewatch, repeat, watch over and over again. The value of circulating these videos appears dubious as liberals and conservatives alike continue to debate the right to life of the person murdered over and over before our eyes. The chasm between seeing a person in pain and in death and the actions it would take to reduce that pain and death is so much wider than the Atlantic.

And so, it seems odd that in 2016, a white artist would not only paint a dead Emmett Till, but opt to hang her dead Emmett Till in 2017 and claim its relevance. In an artist statement updated mid-controversy, Schutz locates the painting's genesis "after a long, violent summer of mass shootings, rallies filled with hate speech, and an ever-escalating number of Black men shot execution style by police, recorded on camera phones as witness." But *Open Casket* disavows the contemporary. Schutz doesn't attend to the ongoing virality of death; she dilates it. It's as if she was without a black friend—statistically probable—or decided to ignore the past one, two, five, twenty years of scholarship and activism to make it plain that she knows best. "There were many reasons why I could not, should not make this painting," she told the *Daily Beast*, before hiding her hand in

Till-Mobley's gesture.[20] "I thought about the possibility of painting it only after listening to interviews with Till's mother. In her sorrow and rage she wanted her son's death not just to be her pain but America's pain."

It's common for white people to reach into the vat of civil rights–era memory to find a racial politics. Only on the subject of race do we permit disregard for intellectual and artistic advancements and address today's problems with yesterday's remedies, like offering lobotomies instead of benzodiazepines. Instead of the spirit of Till-Mobley's activism, Schutz resurrected Bryant and Milam's violence, stroke for stroke. The painting and her words in defense sound nostalgic for a time when the display of America's bad behavior might have been enough to snap some awake, but nostalgia does not make good art. America already eats black pain for dinner and a movie. *Open Casket* says more about the belated nature of Schutz's listening; would that she had explored that matter instead.

New York–based artists Parker Bright and Pastiche Lumumba, strangers before converging at the Whitney, protested the painting on opening day. Bright stood in front of the painting like an intent viewer, his back to other onlookers. His gray T-shirt had "Black Death Spectacle" written in black marker. Lumumba hung a banner outside the museum that read: "The white woman whose lies got Emmett Till lynched is still alive in 2017. Feel old yet?" Lumumba's art in various media considers the experiential implications of context, an expertise relevant to the occasion. He called it "insensitive and gratuitous" for Schutz "to willingly participate in the long tradition of white people sharing and circulating images of anti-black violence."[21] On a 2014 piece of his, a narrow clear strip, like a glass tongue depressor, a motto stands out in bright purple letters: "ART IS A CONTEXT SPORT."

In numerous formats and formalities—from Black's letter to op-eds to tweets and Facebook statuses and hashtags—criticism infiltrated the conversation about a Biennial dedicated above all to avoiding the conversation. Lew and Locks and Schutz and their abundance of allies gave the debate a Socratic blessing, while mobilizing concerns over "censorship" to assert the right to splay a dead boy's remains before the public. Those with at best tenuous commitment to pro-black enterprise acquiesced to the redirected stakes. The critical discussion about who is entitled to racialized pain, refracted by a convex glass called power, resulted in a free speech lesson in which the most entitled get to feel persecuted.

"The painting was never for sale and never will be," Schutz concluded in the updated statement beside the painting. Like Goldsmith shielding his performance from replay, Schutz's choice to remove the painting from circulation looks noble. No doubt the painting would fetch a pretty penny on the market, the controversy netting Schutz a generous uptick in price. But putting circulation on pause is not the same as destruction. As long as the painting exists, it is liable to be passed down, stolen—sold, perhaps, when Schutz reaches an advanced age and no longer cares about a trifling hubbub from a million years ago. And while the physical object remains protected in some storage facility somewhere, its duplicates have already traveled far and wide, entombed by the internet forevermore.

Destruction—so much hand-wringing over the proposal, but only as an ending. Little thought is given to the act of destroying to create. Yet, rupture is required to make that which ought not to exist because it cannot exist without pain onto others. An artist who cannot bear emotional responsibility for their work destroys these others every time they make. It's not enough to hold the art closer. We will never forget. Like the adage about a broken dish, the cracks are m'fucking everything.

And no, she never said sorry.

CHAPTER 4

The Hipster

The New White Negro

In the white man who held him up, Miller recognized a neighbor of his own. After a short detention and a perfunctory search, the white man remarked apologetically:—"Sorry to have had to trouble you, doctuh, but them's the o'ders. It ain't men like you that we're after, but the vicious and criminal class of niggers."

It happens every year. Besides the "Best of" lists that heave into view as early as late November, there are the conspicuous "Worst of" lists. Contrary to their tone, these lists also itemize the things we enjoyed most over the past year, if only too much. These things became part of our daily routine, infiltrated workspaces as well as the home, were used by celebrities, broadcasters, brands, neighbors, and schoolchildren. You might catch them on T-shirts, first from some out-of-nowhere brand sold exclusively on Instagram, then on Etsy, at Forever 21, and finally spotted at New York Fashion Week. You'll hear them in a song, or two or five, a deft handshake with the culture or, more likely, flagging down the eye of Cool. Eventually, the saturation is too much to bear, usually right around the time some politician incorporates the trend for cred among constituents. But they aren't dead yet, not until one final blow. I speak here of words, and our ritual killing of a vocabulary whose greatest sin is popularity.

Worth their weight in clicks, word banishment lists may be found everywhere come the winter holidays, but *Time* magazine once bellowed the loudest. In 2011, as part of a now-defunct "Wednesday Words" column,

Time.com opened a poll asking readers, "What Is 2011's Word of the Year?"
Providing a list of fifteen words including "occupy," "humblebrag," "Arab
Spring," and "winning"—truly a sign o' the times—the rather amiable
question only begged readers to "vote for your favorite words."[1] Barely a
month later the publication was back with another poll, a decidedly more
contentious question in hand: "What word should be *banished* in 2012?"
The query, along with some of the listed options, was borrowed from a
long-running list collected by Michigan's Lake Superior State University
(LSSU), which has been naming words to banish yearly since 1976. *Time's*
list included words such as "baby bump," the prefix "bro-," "sexting," and
hashtags, period.[2] The winner was a trio of acronyms leftover from the
Wild West days of netspeak: OMG, LOL, and WTF.

Though snarky and off-putting in the way much of the internet has
become, the poll offered sound reasons for leaving behind certain turns
of phrase. "Baby bump," for example, invites spectators who monitor
women's bodies, whether the individual in question is indeed pregnant or
bloated or neither (in the resounding words of Queen Cardi B, "Let me
fat in peace"). The prefix "bro," attached to gender-neutral words such as
"romance," "hug," or "crush," allows straight men to safely engage in af-
fectionate behaviors lest they be considered gay or feminine. Adding "bro"
replaces the much harder work of reconsidering the limits of a patriarchy
men otherwise cleave to—that in exchange for power men cannot submit
to one another's company or have a glass of pink wine without a masculine nickname involved (brosé all day, young prince). Another word on
the list, "boss," exemplifies everything awful about the new-millennium
hustle with a dash of corporate feminism according to Sheryl Sandberg.
(Unfortunately for us, the gig economy made sure the fictive liberation of
"be your own boss" wouldn't disappear.)

Time continued its word banishment coverage without incident for
a few more years. The rising 2013 poll included the words "adorkable,"
"artisanal," "cray," and "literally." "YOLO" ("you only live once") won
the title.[3] The 2014 list quarantined "twerk" out of a field with "FOMO,"
"selfie," and "swagger." Then *Time* made a misstep. Jumping the gun in
an early-November 2014 poll, the updated and further antagonistic post
"Which Word Should Be Banned in 2015?" included the word "femi-

nist." The copy speaks in second person, addressing an imaginary reader: "You have nothing against feminism itself, but when did it become a thing that every celebrity had to state their position on whether this word applies to them, like some politician declaring a party? Let's stick to the issues and quit throwing this label around like ticker tape at a Susan B. Anthony parade."[4]

The splashback was enormous, and managing editor Nancy Gibbs offered an apology on behalf of the magazine for the word's inclusion. Within days, "feminist" reached a peak of 51 percent in the pile of "to be banned" words, boosted by campaigns on the misogynist troll nests 4chan and 9gag that encouraged users to vote in favor of its eradication. *Time* never published the final results or announced a winner. It quietly retired its word-banishment program then and there.

LSSU, the alpha and omega of this lexicological affair, soldiered on. Its top nominees that year were "bae," "polar vortex," and "swag," the last noted as receiving "many nominations over the years."[5] Said one submission, from Alex, from Roanoke, Virginia, "I am tired of hearing swag to describe anything on the face of the planet. By the way, your website is 'swag.'"[6] Of another nominee, "cra-cra," Esther from Sault Ste. Marie, Michigan, complained, "I hear kids (including my 6 yr. old) saying it all the time."[7] The words from 2015 to be banned in 2016 led with "conversation," offensive for its invitational quality (i.e., "Join the conversation"); "problematic," deemed either weaselly or whiny; "manspreading," deemed superfluously gendered; and "giving me life," which Anna from Sault St. Marie considered hyperbolic.[8] With *Time* out of the way, other outlets leaped to deliver the secondhand news. "These 13 Annoying Words Are Banned from 2016" read one headline. The Associated Press strung together as many of 2017's words as it could in its lede: "Focus, If You Will, on a Historic, on Fleek Listicle Containing Words Nominated for Bigly Banishment."[9] Words from 2017 and 2018 tell a postelection story as well as anything else, featuring "post-truth," "echo chamber," "disruption," "unpack," "fake news," "gig economy," and "covfefe."[10]

LSSU's Banished Word List has always been an exercise conducted tongue firmly in cheek, as per its full name, "List of Words Banished from the Queen's English for Mis-Use, Over-Use and General Uselessness." Nobody with common sense expects words to evaporate because someone or even a group of someones wants it so. The submissions sound insufferable, but we ought to take stock of our language, at least on occasion. Our clichés say a lot about us. Phrases like "peacekeeping force" or "down time"—on LSSU's 1996 and 1997 lists, respectively—are applied to how we describe the world and ourselves and thus describe what we think we know about the world and ourselves. Some clichés, such as "welfare queen," "axis of evil," and "weapons of mass destruction," encourage a racial perspective that looks truer and truer with each repetition, sounding like something real, as if meaning something apart from the racism whence they came.

But across the forty-three years of LSSU's archive, something disquieting emerges, too. It starts in the '90s, when phrases like "you go, girl" and "da bomb" enter the frame, and later "dawg" and "bling." The common feature of these additions grows more glaring in the 2010's, dramatized by *Time*'s appropriation of LSSU's project. In addition to "feminist," that fateful 2015 list proposed the following for the chopping block: "bae" (shared with LSSU), "basic," "bossy," "disrupt," "I can't even," "influencer," "kale," "literally," "om nom nom nom," "obvi," "said no one ever," "sorry not sorry," "turnt," and "yaaasssss."[11] The list, with few exceptions, curated words derived from black and feminized speech. Only three entries seem genuinely critical of discourse we find ourselves in without notice: "bossy," a common slur against women with expertise and authority; "disrupt," the Silicon Valley motto; and "said no one ever," a sarcastic equal opportunity rejoinder. But the cutified "obvi," "I can't even," "influencer," and "kale" together suggest an immature, girlish archetype worthy of scorn—like young women don't have enough to deal with.

Additionally, the words *Time* draws from black vernacular are attributed to the same archetype, and the magazine doubles down on its obsession with white girls as the harbinger of vernacular trends. "Girls need a word for other girls who name-drop D-listers in their fake Louboutins, going around thinking they're a Carrie, even though they're really a Miranda," reads the hostile copy for "basic," whose meaning black culture made popular.* "Yaaasssss," an expression from ball culture is credited to a viral clip of Lady Gaga. On "bae," another gift from black vernacular: "Yes, this term of endearment has been around for years, but suddenly it's everywhere."[12] Blan, from Sugar Hill, Georgia, was similarly annoyed by its ubiquity when he submitted the term to LSSU. "Also," he added, "the concept 'before anyone else,' developed AFTER the word became popular. Reason enough for it to be banned."[13]

Yes, *insufferable* about fits. For certain words, the complaints rub more acutely, whether they come from a media publication with international reach or a resident of a town whose population barely reaches ten thousand. Neither would know these words enough to be sick of them were it not for the curse destined to hound black culture wherever it goes—the curse of capital-*C* Cool. Whatever new arises in the vernacular can and must be borrowed, replicated, and spun into a marketing slogan of some sort.† The curse is cyclical, like all good curses, for the desires that drive acquisition also immolate the object of desire. Cool isn't *Cool* if everybody does it. The slang once repeated as often as possible is soon pronounced annoying and overused, not by its progenitors but by the very people responsible for its demise. "White Americans often turn on the slang they appropriate, deeming it déclassé or trite after a brief period of infatuation-fueled overuse," journalist and scholar Samantha Allen wrote in an article for the *Daily Beast* during the *Time* controversy.[14] The same phenomenon spurred Todd from Chicago to nominate the death of "bling" in 2004: "This once street slang for items of luxury has now become so overused and abused that (everyone) has incorporated it into their vocabularies. Yes, your mom might say it. Nothing could kill the mystique of a word faster."[15]

The thirst for Cool reappears across the history of American language patterns. "Mickey D's" used to be black slang for the company that now brandishes the name on its billboards. The "Big Apple" was a Depression-era juke brought to New York City. During my childhood, the West Coast's skip-scatting "-eezy" and "-izzle"—commonly associated

---

*Also, like, *what's wrong with being a Miranda*?

†Cue Budweiser's critically acclaimed Whassup? campaign.

with Snoop Dogg, though E-40 claims precedence—bled into everything from Old Navy commercials with Fran Drescher to *Legally Blonde 2: Red, White, and Blonde*. (LSSU elected to banish "'izzle'-speak" in 2005, "by far, the abomination that received the most nominations.")[16] During my mom's childhood, mainstream America learned words like "jive," "kicks," "dig," "bad," "off the hook," and "real." During my Nana's childhood, "hip," "cool," and "chill" made their way to the mouths of a growing white middle class, becoming the common, de-raced lexicon we know them as today. "Now, I do not know what white Americans would sound like if there had never been any black people in the United States," James Baldwin wrote in a 1979 article for the *New York Times*, "but they would not sound the way they sound."[17]

The internet accelerates the process like it accelerates everything. The common send-off "Bye, Felisha" (later shortened to "bye," with "Felisha" left implied) became popular around the mid-2010s, almost two decades after Ice Cube first wrote those lines for the hood classic *Friday*.* Sixteen-year-old Kayla Newman's "on fleek," however, born at the scene of Vine, became popular enough to make banished-words lists within the year. "Woke," the metaphoric term taken up as early as the 1940s as "a call to study and act against anti-black oppression," writes Kashana Cauley, lost its vigor after just a few years of interracial visibility.[18] "Now it functions merely as a nod to the speaker's mainstream lefty positions, a smug confirmation that the speaker holds the expected progressive beliefs," Cauley writes. "What's been left out is any reference to the structural and political systems that caused black leftists to adopt progressivism—or any understanding that maintaining woke views requires continuous work."[19]

Other words come into and fall out of favor at the whim of the viral web. The 2018 internet coalesced around the acronym BDE, for "big dick energy." Reporters rushed to mark its relevance, critics followed to decode its meaning, the usual online boutiques and Etsy shopkeepers and *New*

---

*Google searches for the phrase "Bye Felicia" shot up from 2013 to 2015 and again in 2017. A search result on Etsy shows about a thousand listings for "Bye Felicia" merch. But as a simple IMDB search shows, Deebo's mooch of a girlfriend's name is spelled with *sh*, "Felisha," not "Felicia."

York magazine's *The Cut* sold "BDE" merch. The *Oxford English Dictionary* defined BDE as "an attitude of understated and casual confidence" and added it to the shortlist for 2018 Word of the Year.[20] The music video for Ariana Grande's "thank u, next," already a giddy confluence of digital vernacular and millennial tastes, slapped the letters above the left-side shirt pocket of the distinctive brown uniform in lieu of "UPS." The substitution was more than icing on the ongoing remix of *Legally Blonde* but a nod to the understood origin story of BDE, which overlapped with the rise and aftermath of Ariana's relationship with comedic actor Pete Davidson. While the two were together, Ariana tweeted and deleted her double-digit estimate on the length of her partner's genitalia. This seemed to solve the mystery of her and *him*, not in terms of sexual compatibility but spiritual attraction. If Pete Davidson had a big dick, it made sense, because he carried himself like someone with the comfort of knowing he has a big dick, above the insecure and masculine behavior of one who does not have a big dick, which is ultimately sexier than the dick itself. Or, as Tina Ngo tweeted, "Pete davidson is 6'3 with dark circles, exudes big dick energy, looks evil but apparently is an angel, and loves his girl publicly the only thing wrong w him is that he's a scorpio but anyway . . . id married him within a month too." BDE took off from there, with Ngo, or Ngo's tweet rather, credited with coinage.

In truth the online life of the phrase began with writer Kyrell Grant, who used the term weeks before Ngo, in a tweeted memorial of Anthony Bourdain. "The conversation about Bourdain happened on a night of my friends and I drinking some orange wine and lamenting that none of us would ever get to fuck him, because not only was he hot, he was a man who was very curious and empathetic, and a good listener—which you know is a rare find," she related in *Broadly*.[21] "We came to the conclusion that he must have had a huge dick to match his great personality." She tweeted on June 8, "We're talking about how anthony bourdain had big dick energy which is what he would have wanted." When the phrase took off, Grant was puzzled—"I am largely baffled by the traction of it all, as a whole!"—but wasn't, as had been said in the *Guardian*, "pissed off," until secondhand coverage repeatedly excluded her name, contorting her term in the process.[22] "Others were credited or paid for my work," said Grant.

"It sucks because I made zero dollars from it. Well, almost zero."[23] (*The Cut* shortly discontinued sale of its "BDE" tee, giving Grant the profits, "of about $250.") Eventually, her phrase "got stale the way most memes do: It got repetitive."[24] Grant seemed to mourn the loss of a creative outlet as much as the withheld, or belated, cultural capital. "Honestly, I think I've already phased out using Twitter for any of my better observations. . . . The mindset that the discovery of an idea is akin to creating it is something that's too embedded in all of us, and I don't think it's going away."[25]

Another case study: "chile." Camped out on the behemoth social aggregate site Reddit—more specifically on a subforum of beauty industry gossip—I see an exchange that makes my stomach hurt. The context of the exchange matters little; it was merely one node in the rapidly unfolding timeline of rumor upon rumor coherent to local users who live for mess. The conversation went as follows:

> USER 1: If [username] picks the story up, CHILE. . . .
> USER 2: "CHILE." What does this mean? I'm not hip to the slang anymore.
> USER 3: It's slang for "child."
> USER 4: It's AAVE slang specifically, to my knowledge.
> USER 1: ♥ ♥ ♥ love you addressed it as AAVE
> USER 1: CHILE can be perceived as "girl, this drama is going be good"

"Chile." The eternal feature of black Southern speech survived its transport to the North and elsewhere by way of the Great Migration only to be hacked into pieces by the internet. Confused User 2 calls it slang; User 3 concurs; User 4 doubles down in the most incorrect politically correct way—"AAVE slang." The qualified smug—"specifically, to my knowledge"—deflates for noting "AAVE slang" lengthens to "African American Vernacular English slang" (gibberish). The absurdity compounds for noting that confused User 2 (correctly) incorporates a loan from black vernacular—"hip"—to express their misrecognition. User 1 did nothing wrong but nobody comes out unscathed.

"Chile" is neither new nor slang. There is a popular meme pulled from the Bravo reality show *The Real Housewives of Atlanta*, part of the franchise about working women showing women at work. In the relevant scene, Nene Leakes, the show's star and an original cast member, visits cast mate Kenya Moore at her temporary lodgings in an undisclosed hotel in downtown Atlanta. As Nene steps out of her Range Rover, she huffs, "Whew, chile, the ghetto! The ghetto. The ghetto." It's an exaggeration, the exact tenor of comedic airs that viewers come to expect from Nene, *the* master of the *Real Housewives* format, which thrives on the illusion of monetary insouciance while exhibiting the most class-obsessed characters you'll find on TV. In meme form, the phrase and its various abbreviations became applicable to any situation giving one the slightest grief: going though regular airport security instead of TSA PreCheck, *Whew, chile . . . the ghetto*; standard shipping instead of Prime delivery, *Whew, chile . . . the ghetto*; low water pressure, *Whew, chile . . .* As the catchphrase detached from the original clip, "Whew, chile" encountered audiences unfamiliar with the sound and cadence of this very black, very Southern exhalation. Some wondered what the country west of Argentina has to do with anything. In a video on Twitter, user Cameron Collins captures his own shock while an offscreen voice begs to know, "How do you say woo, chilé . . . woo, chilé," adding an accented second syllable. *Chillay* became such a hit that many black millennials reappropriated it for themselves, exclaiming "Whew, chillay" on- and offline where "Whew, chile" once was. Sometimes there's nothing left to do but laugh.

Between the yearly kill lists, explainers for the darnnedest things kids are saying, the genre of works that frustrated Grant, elide blackness by ignorance or by choice with identical results. When "basic" hit the mainstream, one long-running magazine called it an "epithet" against femininity. One new-media site described "basic" as an expression of class anxiety. Another site offered readers a glossary for terms like "lit," "fam," "woke," "tea," "lowkey," and "receipts," omitting the black and queer origins of what it also called "internet slang." Another online magazine gave the word "washed" similar treatment, equating the expression with "cool." There again is the repeated irony—the cultural roots erased from one term by another term, "cool," whose blackness got lost on mainstream audiences.

Language does and does not conform to the sorts of top-down and oppressive boundaries imposed by humans in power. Language lives in people. As people interact and change, so, too, will the means they use to communicate ideas and feelings. Barriers to change include geography, which for centuries guarded, for example, the Gullah language of the Geechee people on the Southern coasts; or in the pre-internet world kept black speech slow to dissipate from enclaves on the plantation, the ghetto, and the *inner city*. The United States has never been totally segregated, but this new world exposes everyone to everyone else in unprecedented intensity. Just like we sound like our friends, just like someone with a new friend group will inevitably find bits of new language and inside jokes slipped into their own speech, vernacular from here and there and wherever sneaks into conversations between people who've never been to those places.

The appropriation of black language cannot be stopped, except only if we were to leave for Mars and never come back. At issue isn't the transmission, but the vacuous want behind it—as if black culture lives to rescue mass culture from boredom. Surely there exists some ethical method for taking on the words of others—white America has yet to find it. For the curse to be undone, the desire must be undone, and undoing the desire means taking a knife to its insides and learning what it's full of.

Norman Mailer's 1957 essay "The White Negro" is not about what I assume most readers expect it's about once they get down to the business of reading. Mailer uses the formulation "white Negro" exactly once aside from in the title, and he uses it for descriptive, not taxonomic, purpose:

> So there was a new breed of adventurers, urban adventurers who drifted out at night looking for action with a black man's code to fit their facts. The hipster had absorbed the existentialist synapses of the Negro, and for practical purposes could be considered a white Negro.[26]

The distinction between description and taxonomy is important. Across the six-part essay, Mailer isn't interested in problematizing the hipster so much as psychologizing him. He reassembles the contemporary world in order to understand why America's promising young white men would seek the slums, speak in strange tenses, and look to their suburban future as a fate worse than dying young. His answer is totalitarianism, by exactly that name, but also whiteness. Both are parasitic relations to the world that kill everything in their path and rot the insides of their hosts.

World War II forms the backdrop of his investigation. The war and all its accoutrements: concentration camps, chemical warfare, and the United States' agent of instantaneous genocide called the atom bomb. These atrocities left their witnesses changed, including the ones secluded in pleasant suburbs, enjoying the wealth the war brought home. And herein arose one of many "insoluble contradictions" divined to drive young white men mad.[27] "If society was so murderous," wrote Mailer, "then who could ignore the most hideous of questions about his own nature?" If the same society that made war and all its evils also made man, then no man is exempt from the evil that grows inside him.

In Mailer's terms, the hipster yearns to live dangerously so that he—Mailer uses exclusively masculine pronouns for his hipsters—may rewire his instincts, afore dulled by the gray monotony of white American life. Cultural theft is only the symptom, the readily identifiable mark of whiteness in crisis. The hipster yearns, as his parents never did, to reconcile his place in the violently modern society that could at any moment see him dead *with* the inheritance that would see him at the helm of the same violent society if all goes to plan. The hipster seeks out "the Negro" because from who better to learn the transitive properties of living than the community who could never take life for granted?

"So it is no accident that the source of Hip is the Negro for he has been living on the margin between totalitarianism and democracy for two centuries," writes Mailer, in a statement as true in the new millennium as it was in the postwar '50s.[28] And his disillusioned but energized white youth share much with today's teenagers (and the teenage at heart). Then, they latched on to the jazzman, a "cultural mentor of a people" who spoke in a special way that, like his music, communicated the experience of a person who was always, at least psychically, on the run from something. I observed the same impulse growing up in a Midwest suburb an hour from the city: adolescents, white, angry, and usually (but not always) male, injured by some slight dealt them, apparently, from the womb, hating their mothers, resenting their fathers, losing themselves in Dre and Biggie, black men with thick voices, until they found their patron saint, the angry and white (and poor) Marshall "Eminem" Mathers, whose equivalent to-day might be the mellower Post "White Iverson" Malone. Hip-hop *is* the culture now, a guiding light for white teens and twenty-somethings and thirty-somethings and beyond of whatever gender, scared of the world, looking for a language to live in. Which brings me to *nigga*.

At a festival performance, the Pulitzer-awarded Kendrick Lamar invited a white fan onstage to test her chops performing "M.A.A.D. City," a song off his debut studio album. The woman, Delaney, knew the words well enough and pronounced them clearly—all of them, including *nigga*, which punctuates the end of each phrase. Kendrick put her on pause, but gave Delaney another chance. "You gotta bleep one single word, though," he warned. Delaney whined. "Am I not cool enough for you? What's up, bro?" she asked. "I'm used to singing this like I wrote it." This exchange, relayed to the world by blurry cell-phone footage, gave me another stomachache.

Language doesn't conform to rules or boundaries or borders. Anyone who would call it a stroke of unprecedented luck that a weapon of white supremacy could flower in our hands hasn't looked around and seen what black people in America have made of chains and redlined neighborhoods, pigs' feet, catfish, and collards (before they were cool). Unlike some other slurs, *nigga* sits on the tongue like butter. It rhymes with almost anything, nothing better than itself, as the opening lines to "M.A.A.D. City" demonstrate. It may be softened with an *a* or hardened with an *r* and an accent to comic effect. (Can anything in the history of mankind be funnier than Dave Chappelle, ashy, blind, and preaching against "naggers," playing the role of the black white supremacist Clayton Bigsby?) *Nigga* is grand in every way but one: from the mouths of the nonblack ones, who oddly enough have the hardest time letting go.

It's generally understood that the meanings behind words are subject to change over time. "Gay," once a common synonym for blissful, now more usually refers to someone attracted to the same gender. "Queer" meant odd, then became a slur for anyone outside a heteronormative lifestyle, and was then mobilized by those anyones as an affirmation for radical living. "Awesome" has become more pedestrian than sublime, and "literally" has linked arms with its former opposite, "figuratively," a definition that's made its way into *Merriam-Webster's*.*

But when we think of the evolution of a word, it is best not to assume this new definition replaces the old. As we're already in the practice of comparing words to plants it makes much more sense to think of them as trees with roots and branches where each branch is another possibility for meaning that exists in relation to other meanings. And if one of those branches once provided so many switches with which to strip humanity from generations of people, we can't assume that branch has rotted off and died simply because another, unexpected branch has grown up and out from the same mother tree. "Nigger," like so many other racial, gendered, and sexual slurs, hasn't lost any branches yet.

White and nonblack people who defend their right to use *nigga* in public generally don't intend to use it pejoratively (in public, at least). Self-aware racists usually keep quiet. This isn't their fight. White people who defend their right to use *nigga* want the right to hop to another branch without the memory of the branch left behind. They don't want the "nigger" of their ancestors and relatives, but the *nigga* known to their rap idols. Of course, they forget that *nigga* wouldn't be *nigga* without the vulgar thrills encrusted upon it. Danger always accompanies anything genuinely hip, and nothing is more hip than *nigga*. If it wasn't dangerous, white people wouldn't want it.

The "who can say it" conversation, resurrected every couple months or so when a public figure (Paula Deen, Bill Maher, "Papa" John Schnatter) says something stupid, sidesteps reality in more ways than one, but especially in the plethora of opportunities white people have, right now, today, to say *nigga*. White people say *nigga* all the time—in cars, in bars. Had

---

*Much to the chagrin of self-appointed "grammar Nazis" who *surprisingly* haven't read their Saussure.

Delaney decided to sit this one out and rap-yell by herself in a crowd of thousands, she could have said the word to her heart's content. White people do so at every rap show, one of the reasons why I don't have too much fondness for rap shows above a certain price level and venue capacity. Part of me wonders if it's not a small unadvertised incentive for white people to attend concerts. Sometimes it seems like they love that word more than the lyrical bars that contain it. More than the songs. More than rap music.

If there is something broken in all of us—and there must be, living in a world like this—that is true in triplicate for white people, who must observe so much of the world's evil enacted by people with whom they share a face. Today is no less scary than yesterday—the bombs are more devastating, the wars are ongoing, and the intelligence speaks back to us from the living room, turning *1984* into quaint historical fiction. Everyone is scared shitless, but the good liberal white person cannot bear to disavow friends and family, cannot dare the smallest confrontation at Thanksgiving dinner and so looks for freedom elsewhere. Liberal white Americans still suppose black people might be the key to the gateway away from conformity, the "normal," boring life too quiet to drown out the screams of sorrow and agony required to maintain a normal, boring life in the twenty-first century. Speaking the language of hip, learning it on their tongue, seems one step closer to *being interesting* and distinct from their upbringing and destiny. White people speak black to feel alive—to feel *real*.

And maybe, just maybe, that feeling can become reality. Mailer knew the hipster to be a shallow pose, but one that could, if pushed, yield "a radical comprehension of the horror of society."[29] The outcome would be up to the hipsters, the liberal generation seeking refuge in black scenes. As Mailer foresaw, black Americans would continue to acquire rights and something more like citizenship as the decades wore on. What happened from there meant everything. Would an appreciation for capital-*H* Hip see these new citizens being incorporated into America harmoniously? Would liberals express fondness for black people as equals? Or, will their discomfort grow upon seeing black life moving inward from the margins? Will they resent sharing sidewalks and offices and classrooms, competing for affluence the same way they've competed only with other white people since time immemorial? Will they smash their records, lose their loose tongue, and hide in the safe cocoon of whiteness while the fight for rights rages outside their door?

> A time is coming when every political guide post will be gone, and millions of liberals will be faced with political dilemmas they have so far succeeded in evading, and with a view of human nature they do not wish to accept.[30]

Ronald Reagan won forty-four states in 1980, so we know how that story went.

I ponder the same questions as white America approaches another precipice, with no answer more plausible than any other. Will love for rap music soar into oblivion while gentrification and climate change make black life untenable? Will white teens still outsource their charity? Will white parents still prefer a $4,000 plane ticket to the heart of darkness over a dollar bill to the homeless? Will the writer bold enough to say "appropriation" online speak up the next time Daddy says "nigger"? Will the fast-food joint living fat off R&B and g-droppin' let free meat and potatoes rain over deserted neighborhoods?

Would that black people could put a price on linguistic faculties and charge rent for how much space our words take up in others' heads. The profits would be spectacular. Premiums for *nigga* would be sky-high and cost extra on Wednesdays, just because. We'd buy each other out of poverty and pay our way to near-perfect SAT scores and prestigious internships just like they do. *Woulda coulda shoulda.*

No, now as then the imperative rests with the ones whose behavior needs to change if we are to hope for an end to that merry-go-round, talking the talk and walking a whole other walk entirely. It is not anything to sound one voice if there's no love in it. Black speech cannot sooth the broken white soul. Only revolution can do that.

Until then, I'll be working on that rocket.

PART III

Technology

CHAPTER 5

The Meme

Kermit the Frog Meets Nina Simone

*"Josh—men—you are throwing your lives away. It
is a fever; it will wear off to-morrow, or to-night."*

Crying Jordan executed the comeback of Michael's dreams. This nugget, or creature more like, emblematic of all this country's potent anxieties, was for years an inescapable feature of life online. When Derrick Rose returned after tearing the ACL in his left knee just to tear the meniscus in his right a month later, Crying Jordan was there. When the Houston Rockets fell to Golden State in the playoffs, 2016 in this case, Crying Jordan was there, copied a dozen times in miniature to cover the entirety of James Harden's trademark beard. When Villanova piccoloist Roxanne Chalifoux cried during an upset in the 2015 NCAA Men's Basketball Tournament, Crying Jordan was there. Crying Jordan was there for the winningest quarterback after a two-point loss to Peyton Manning's Broncos; he was there when it was announced that a new twenty-dollar bill would demote a slaveholding paternalist in favor of a gun-toting liberator.* He was there for Halloween masks and Powerball numbers, on a fictional but apropos cover for *Time*'s Person of the Year. And then he disappeared, Airbender fashion, during the eve of the 2016 election, right when we needed him most.

---

*Plans for the renovated bill halted as soon as Donald Trump took office.

Perhaps the fun had run out. Perhaps he'd been thinkpiece'd to death, clumsily autopsied by the likes of austere magazines who only yesterday discovered online life as something worth serious attention. Perhaps the Adobe free trials of some key players expired, mysteriously, at the same time. Perhaps, having traveled far, far from Springfield, Massachusetts, the site of Jordan's now-infamous Hall of Fame induction speech in 2009, and exhausted of his labors, Crying Jordan had clocked out just in time to let some other idiom do its fair share. The virtual object virtually disappeared, leaving a chaos of symbols in its wake.

Not a year and a half later, Crying Jordan reappeared. He came in the face of the chaplain for Loyola University's men's basketball team, a ninety-eight-year-old named Sister Jean. She'd become something of a mascot for the Cinderella team's run in the 2018 Tournament. But in the semifinals, the No. 3–seed Wolverines quite defeated the No. 11–seed Ramblers 69–57, prompting fairy tale to become farce. Jordan's face slipped behind the devout lady's silver wired frames, baldness replaced by white fuzz; a particularly ruthless version relocates the varsity letter from her jacket to her hands, compelling Crying Sister Jean Jordan to "hold the '*L*'" as it were. Crying Jordan, returned. Just like that.

To appreciate the magnificence, the sheer chef's kiss of it all requires a certain fluency in the grammar of the contemporary internet. To understand how a digital cutout superseded the ubiquity of a man so iconic the greatest ballplayer of all time still dances with his memory, one must come to know these units of culture that exceed their digital prisms, that are as much a part of *real life* as anything else online: memes. And knowing memes means knowing the internet as irrevocably black as fuck.

Memes are fickle, mysterious. Another tale: Mid-February 2016, a tan, besneakered high school student named Daniel captivated the internet. He had been captured in a compilation of Vine-like Snapchats walking about what appears to be school grounds, sporting various versions of what might best be called SoCal floppy-hair chic. Often caught mid-stride, moving about or backing away from the camera, Daniel cuts a playfully bashful figure, laughing not to the camera but meeting eyes with an unseen cameraman who interjects into each video a raspy "Daaamn, Daniel!" Though Daniel makes a charming avatar, that recitation, from fellow student Josh Holz, became the star of the show. Within the days the catchphrase went viral. Parodies soon appeared, leaping from Twitter to the actual Vine platform, the ideal medium for impossibly brief narrative shorts. One, uploaded by a user named cursilano and simply titled "Damn, Daniel," was "looped" (viewed) over 1.8 million times. It dubs in Holz's voice over video of a smiling, bearded man wearing an approximate Daniel costume (backpack and all). The camera pans down just as Holz laughingly finishes the long-form version of the catchphrase, which includes the addendum, "Back at it again with the white Vans!" referring to Daniel's bright slip-on kicks. In the parody, "Daniel" thuds across the pavement, feet encased in what are revealed to be twin plastic toy minivans (painted white, of course).

The fanfare only intensified from there. Eager to monetize whatever the kids are up to, brands seized on the chance to be hip to the moment. Clorox gave the meme a new tagline, "Damn, Daniel: Get back at it again with Clorox," tweeting a photo of dirty white sneakers that look suspiciously like Chuck All-Stars. Someone drew up an emoji of a white sneaker for the occasion. Vans, naturally, embraced the limelight. A brand could do worse than arrive at a viral marketing campaign on the fly.* After eight days online, the video netted fourteen-year-old Daniel Lana a lifetime supply of Vans and an appearance on *Ellen*, *the* media slot synonymous with viral stardom. Months later *Bloomberg* reported a double digit boost in sales for the apparel company.† And then, *just like that*, Damn, Daniel was gone. He would not return.

Every day, images, sounds, and phrases are lost and found in the ever overturning lifecycle(s) of internet culture. Memes "go viral," leaving their niche (an NBA forum or Riverdale Poly High School) to circulate within the reach of others who will adapt and remix the original as they

---

*Later that year, Red Lobster would bungle the opportunity to capitalize on lyrics in "Formation" after Beyoncé's surprise video release.

†Some speculated that Damn, Daniel might have been planted as part of a guerrilla marketing campaign, but Vans denies any involvement. (Lindsey Rupp, "'Damn, Daniel!' You Sold a Lot of White Shoes," *Bloomberg*, April 29, 2016.)

see fit. Passive participants might prefer to only retweet (Twitter) or reblog (Tumblr) or upvote (Reddit) or repost (Instagram) the memes that speak to their humor or experience, but their role is not unimportant. Every share is an opportunity for a meme to find a new audience and mutate once again. One Oscars night, Crying Jordan underwent the most stunning transfiguration. After the academy's long neglected son received the award for Best Actor for *The Revenant*, the user @whoisjoserivera tweeted the famous photo of Jordan mid-soar during his famous free-throw-line dunk from the 1988 contest, Jordan's head replaced by Leo's as he looked in the film. (The tweet's caption, "Not today, the internet," borrowed from another viral phenomenon, uttered by *RuPaul's Drag Race* season six winner Bianca Del Rio. "Not today, Satan," has a meme life all its own, in gifs and on mugs, key chains, necklaces, and T-shirts in a swoopy, Pinterest-friendly font.)

So goes the livelihood of a meme. By fate or like magic, some memes manage to extend their existence for what feels like eons in an online arena where ad nauseam is an understatement. Some memes, like Crying Jordan, are too attuned to our baser sensibilities to ever truly fade from view (isn't there always a loser worth ribbing?). Out of all the nostalgia-inducing 'toons from Nickelodeon's past, *SpongeBob SquarePants* won the post-2010s internet, becoming the source of countless viral memes. Another unexpected childhood fixture, Kermit the Frog, regularly appears in memes and reaction images.[*] After LeBron James led the Cleveland Cavaliers to their first championship title, he Instagrammed a selfie with the Larry O'Brien trophy, his head pulled down to show off a baseball cap embroidered with a small portrait of Kermit sipping tea from a mug. The hat and his caption's parting words—"That's None of My Business"—pettily cites a popular meme that pivots the Southern charmer into a messy gossip. Kermit literally sips his Lipton—the image pulled from a 2014 ad spot—while the text around him spills figurative "tea," a word from queer culture for covert speech or gossip. Elsewhere run rampant images of counterfeit Kermit-like green frogs drinking,

---

[*] His only rival is Tiffany Pollard. Reaction images are still images or gifs used to illustrate a certain expression or emotion.

dabbing, wrapped in blankets, touching hands in the mirror, and otherwise pondering the meaning of existence. Even the green frog emoji has acquired new significance.

Not everyone can be Jordan or Kermit. Memes more commonly resemble Damn, Daniel, surging and flaming out, supernova style. After weeks of nonstop fun, after cable news covers it, after the T-shirts are made, but before standard shipping and handling has them at anyone's doorstep, the meme exhausts its cause. And its cause is pleasure, nothing more. 'Tis the frenzy that ushers their demise.* And we accept the internet's flighty nature same as we assume we will only know its rhythms in the aftermath and not a moment sooner. Never has a tech journalist with the unfortunate task of covering the now bona fide internet culture beat ever scooped a previously unknown meme—she must instead chase after memes, belatedly, like a paparazzo. What else to be done with sixty-year-old Muppets and twenty-year-old aardvarks and three-year-old rap battles up for grabs? When the five-year-old nephew of a Vine star (yep) might just be the lovable mascot for millennials' everyday existential crises?† Nothing makes sense after you log on.

For the confusion over the term he created we might blame Richard Dawkins, ethnologist, evolutionary biologist of sorts, and living specter. Before fathering a generation of Islamophobic white men who consider atheism a personality trait, Dawkins, in his 1976 book *The Selfish Gene*, coined the word "meme" to describe components of culture that survive, propagate, and die off just as genes do. Though Dawkins has yet to return to the subject in earnest, the study, which extends evolutionary theory to cultural development, spawned an entire field dedicated to studying memes: memetics. Memetics is generally uninterested in *why* these components survive, or the contexts that allow them to do so—much as individual persons are considered unwitting actors within the gene pool at large, so, too, are our motivations deemed irrelevant when it comes to the transmission of culture.

---

*Dearly Beloved, We gather here today to mourn the passing of these fair memes: Dat Boi, Salt Bae, queer Babadook, PawPaw . . .

†Gavin, the only good and pure thing to be found online.

Much like Dawkins himself, memetics has attracted substantial criticism from researchers skeptical of the field's scientific rigor. And memes-as-genes looks absurd in an online context where the word "meme" bypasses the reach of Dawkins's imagination. By his capacious definition, memes may be sayings, bass lines, accents, myths, a design pattern, or a style of body modification. Counterintuitively, the internet gives memes more structure and formal constraints, a grammar. Memes are more akin to jokes—a phrase, often coupled with an image, that follows a certain format within which adjustments can be made before being redistributed to amuse others. Anthropologist Elise Kramer has discussed how jokes take on a sacred, untouchable quality in culture. They are deemed inexplicable—just watch friends' faces fall when you ask them to explain the humor in the joke they've just made. "The person who spends too much time mulling over a joke is accused of ruining it," says Kramer.[1] Memes are similar. We don't want to know what they say about us. We want to chuckle and move on.

The people in charge of the apps where memes live prefer not to think about us. The tech industry prefers not to think of humans. Facebook sells users like the products we are. Twitter chooses to think of harassers as bots instead of dangerous racists. YouTube allows white supremacist conspiracies to thrive, even after these videos prove formative to murder sprees all over the world. Uber maintains its status as an app rather than a livery service, avoiding pesky lower-order concerns like workers' compensation or the frequent sexual assaults enabled by the platform. Tech devours any and all signs of human agency: the Bay Area thus transformed into a dystopian refuge for the obscenely wealthy, Silicon Valley at its hellish core. Aside from the handful of white billionaires whose names are conditioned to memory, anonymity is the last word. The devices we hold *just happen* and the things on our screens *just happen.* From this perspective, memes acquire lives of their own, overriding the people involved in the cultural phenomenon that—for now—needs people to exist. "That the speed and relative borderlessness of the internet makes cross-platform, global dissemination seem like a consequence of tech is a convenient amnesia," the critic Doreen St. Félix surmises, thinking about black kids gone viral in *The Fader,* an online magazine.[2] Gestures to the zeitgeist as the end of curiosity makes the ghostliness created by forgetting visible.

There's blackness in that ghostliness. Not in terms of ownership—black folks are hardly the sole proprietors of memes, nor, I think, would anyone want to be. As jokes, as linguistic morphemes or sacred texts, memes thrive for being shared and experienced among the many, not the few. Yet, still, something in the way they move models experiments tested by black vernacular some time ago. Memes at their liveliest look indebted to very black processes of cultural survival.

Black people are the best part of going online. Black culture is the fiber in the memes that are sometimes the only reasonable excuse for logging on while the world crumbles. Memes not only contain components of black language, not only gravitate toward a black way of speaking, but also in their circulation latch on to black cultural modes of improvisation to move through space and subsist in an ultracompetitive visual-verbal environment. The way memes change, adapt, fold into themselves, make old like new is *black asf.*

This point exudes essentialisms. "Black language"? "*Black* way of speaking"? Not all black people talk the same, you say, and that's true. Black people don't even speak the same colonial and indigenous languages from nation to nation, let alone have one universal tongue among the race that includes thousands of ethnicities and cultures spanning every continent on Earth.* Meanwhile, voices differ even within a unit as tight as family—Keisha talks like the aunties from work, Damon has a slight lisp, Michelle, home from study abroad, speaks in wannabe Italian.

White people, imperceptive when it comes to variations in black folks' speech, are irritating enough. Race talk loves a visual metaphor, yet race, too, has been sonically monitored for centuries. Building on W. E. B. Du Bois and his theory of the "color line," Jennifer Lynn Stoever, a professor of English at SUNY Binghamton, calls the racial borders of sound the "sonic color line."[3] On the white side of this line are people who do not come together with more than maybe one black person at a time,

---

*George Washington Gibbs Jr. became the first person of African descent to set foot in Antarctica in 1939, at least as far as we know.

people who do not socialize with black people, people whose black friend does not count them as one, people who are unaccustomed to hearing a black person speak off-television—almost any white person fits this description. And so white people interpret black voices with all the racial baggage that accrues around black bodies, whether or not a black person is present. Certain dialects, vocal ranges, and vernacular are deemed noisy, improper, or hyperemotional by association with blackness. White people "hear themselves as 'normal' citizens," says Stoever, while anything black or assumed black is deviant (ask Michael Dunn).* In *Bring the Pain*, his 1996 HBO special, Chris Rock chides the way white people compliment Colin Powell: "He speaks so well!" The backhanded comment is familiar. "What voice were you looking to come out of his mouth? What the fuck did you expect him to sound like?" Rock puts on the minstrel. "I'm a drop a bomb today. I be pre-zo-dent!"

When I speak of black language, I'm uninterested in stereotypes, at least insofar as reckoning with stereotypes often involves hypercorrection in the other direction, proving over and over again the "not like that" of it all, missing the critical detail that stereotypes exist because of white power and not the other way around. (As the great Ayesha A. Siddiqi once said, "Stop trying to fact check fascism and fight it.") If thinking about black language pries open the innards of what constitutes culture— where does it live, what are the boundaries, what happens when it no longer lives in the same place or looks like what it was—closure would be no fun at all. More fascinating than stereotypes are the astounding similarities across time and space, brought all the closer by twentieth- and twenty-first-century migrations (West Africa to Europe, the West Indies to Canada, East Africa to Canada, West Africa to the Caribbean to Europe, American South to North, American South to West, West Indies to American North, the Caribbean to South Florida, South America to South Florida, Central America to the South . . .), brought closer still by

---

*In 2012 forty-five-year-old Michael Dunn—white—shot and killed a black teenager named Jordan Davis at a Jacksonville, Florida, gas station. Dunn attacked Davis and his friends for playing music in their car. Dunn's fiancée, Rhonda Rouer, testified in court that Dunn told her, "I hate that thug music" shortly before the murder. (Rick Neale, "Dunn Retrial: Jury Hears from Former Fiancée," *USA Today*, September 28, 2014.)

an online sense of diaspora. Words differ, accents differ, styles differ, the pop culture artifacts that move us differ. Yet black peoples, in shared exile from the kingdom of culture, devise modes of expression that flourish under constant surveillance.

In the 1970s, research on blackness in America was saddled with the need to dispute pervasive myths about black culture. And still, black Americans are looked upon as the almost-but-not-quite-assimilated descendants of Africans who arrived as the alleged tabula rasa for the absorption of European beliefs and expressive forms. For scholars, responses to this intellectual legacy meant asserting, contrary to both fin-de-siècle grammarians and later post-segregationist educational policy, that black language is a linguistic category in and of and for itself: a coherent derivation of West African language forms, patterned into adopted (but not bastardized) English.

In the decades since, some researchers have usefully loosened that insistence on a black language standard. US-centrism at leading research institutions leaves studies of black vernacular in English overrepresented compared to other phonetic traditions, with white American researchers as overrepresented authors of that work. In many cases motivated by state-led educational imperatives and what's euphemistically called "the black-white achievement gap," studies that insist upon the autonomy of black English still find themselves in too much of a hurry to reach a results-based objective to hang out with the variables that give any type of people their nuances from place to place. For, black language can be black and also occur specifically in dialects, patois, and creoles among peoples with generational, geographical, political, and cultural differences. For, not every black person speaks every vernacular, the vernacular isn't limited to just black people, and its resemblance to otherwise precariously bounded languages may tell us less than we think about how it resides in people.

This messiness resounds on all sides in my use of the term "black language": a language that lives in people, even when those people operate within the bodiless abandon of cyberspace. Black language as much ascribes a community as a grammar; is a diction, a style, a politics all at once. Within networks of peoples unified but by no means defined by racialization, black language is spoken, written, gestured, intuited, and invented. Its innovations arise within those networks, destined to (re)surface and disperse.

In her seminal 1977 study *Talkin and Testifyin: The Language of Black America*, Professor Geneva Smitherman describes Nina Simone's sung "it bees dat way sometime" as a "total expression" of "Black English style."[4] There is the habitual verb "be," which houses a grammatical, temporal function. Then there is the "method" or perspective of the statement entire that reflects an enduring cultural refrain among a people continuously marginalized in *this* way in *this* space.

How "it bees dat way sometime" in 1967 is also "it be like that sometimes" in the new millennium is also indicative of black style.* Retaining a certain grammar says more than the grammar itself. More than the exact words, it is all about the layering of meaning accumulated over decades in a phrase that has stayed yet has moved, transformed into the similar and different "it be like that" feeling that's so *now* and so old at the same time. The process is shared by language and culture at large and explains how it takes a four-hundred-year remove for English students to struggle with diction and syntax. How fashion of the early twenty-tens looks a lot like a return to the '90s with a twist. How earnest slang from the past resurges semi-ironically in the now: "dope," "clutch," "down," "jam."

Even though, by definition, anything called culture is constantly in a patchwork process of (re)making itself with old material, the survivalist maneuver is enacted most skillfully by traditions that know themselves to be up for grabs, that must always be made anew but never lose spirit. The spirit of black expression inflects these things called memes that move about the world as if they, too, are constantly surveilled (which they in fact are). Their mutations might be the matter of fact of a competitive environment, but maybe of a more benevolent, communal one as well. People often combine memes. In one Vine, Daniel's bashful fashion show

---

*Or, in the historic words attributed to baseball's Oscar Gamble, "They don't think it be like it is, but it do." (Gamble quoted in Dan Epstein, *Big Hair and Plastic Grass: A Funky Ride Through Baseball and America in the Swinging '70s* [reprint, New York: St. Martin's/ Griffin, 2012], p. 182.)

cuts to a popular vine featuring someone named Aaron, who tumbles into a suspended Krispy Kreme sign, creating the fused "back at it again . . . at Krispy Kreme."* Like little remixes, combined memes use each other but also help each other by enhancing their most empathetic qualities—making new within the impossible speed of the internet. Their mixing and merging is evidence of a human touch, a glimpse of a more improvisational moment. A black moment.

Inaugurating a *very* black moment, Vine began much like any other social network, and not until its demise was it realized what would be missed. Founded in 2012 by a trio of entrepreneurs—a word often, as also here, applied to men with some coding knowledge and access to obscene amounts of money—Vine initiated the bite-size video format, a home for looping uploads each six seconds max. To the extent that Facebook altered our relation to friendship and Twitter, to sustained thought, Vine changed online video, hitting the viral sweet spot. Twitter, incidentally, acquired the platform shortly before it launched in 2013 and shut it down three years later when Vine proved unable to turn itself into a money tree. In those three years, millions of users making millions of videos looped millions of times took Vine's limitations in their teeth and named themselves artisans of a new form. Vine became a "unique incubator," as *The Fader*'s Jordan Darville put it, its influences felt across the web.[5] "Watching the community and the tool push on each other was exciting and unreal, and almost immediately it became clear that Vine's culture was going to shift towards creativity and experimentation," Dom Hofmann, one of its founders, told *The Verge*.[6]

Apps often come and go in a poof of VC lack of interest, but Vine felt different. Vine was mourned. More visibly than anywhere else, Vine rewarded the often comedic storytelling of its popular black users. As "both its own ecosystem of cultural production and an engine that powers cross-platform social media trends," wrote Hannah Giorgis in the

---

*I call it "meme merge," this tendency for users to compel memes to collaborate and absorb one another.

Guardian, Vine both came into its own through black comedy and also needed black comedy to make itself bigger than a mobile app, which for a time was the only way into Vineworld.[7]

And the demise of the app wasn't inevitable. In 2015, over a dozen of Vine's most popular creators met with executives from Vine and Twitter to propose what would have been a mutually beneficial solution to the app's financial concerns. "If Vine would pay all 18 of them $1.2 million each, roll out several product changes and open up a more direct line of communication," Taylor Lorenz reported, "everyone in the room would agree to produce 12 pieces of monthly original content for the app, or three vines per week."[8] If Vine declined to pay these creators for further works put on the app, the group would walk off the app entirely. One of their requests in the way of product changes included effective guards against harassment. "Several viners said the community had taken a negative turn and their comments had turned into buckets of abuse," wrote Lorenz. Most of the Viners who came to the table were not black, but the meeting's outcome would say much about this tech company's felt responsibility to compensate a group of people bringing life to its platform(s). The success of these Viners' rescue attempt had implications for the many more mid- to upper-tier Viners—many of them black—who introduced so much of America, so much of the world, to their homegrown brand of tomfoolery.

The meeting's outcome is obvious: Vine is gone. "This was a rare case when creative Internet labor was organized enough and held enough leverage to negotiate collectively," writes author Malcolm Harris, "but the important lesson from the story is that platforms would rather disappear entirely than start collective bargaining with talent."[9]

Vines went extinct, yet the ghost of Internet cool still haunts us. Someone might still prompt their friend, "Watch this vine," even if the video is ten seconds or two minutes long. Twitter, Facebook, YouTube, and Instagram remain rife with compilations of creative content made for Vine for free by artists, comedians, and other storytellers. New slogans sprang into common speech, here forever. In one video, looped millions of times, an adorable child breaks into dance after being urged for the third time to "do it for the vine." It inspired a slew of remakes long before Damn, Daniel hit the scene. In what must be the most influential Vine of all time, Peaches Monroee, a.k.a Kayla Newman, admires her brows in the front-facing camera, declaring them "on fleek."

Though "on fleek" was everywhere—Hefty ads, tweets from Denny's and Taco Bell, fast fashion crop tops—Newman did not get the *Ellen* treatment or a lifetime supply of anything. "I gave the world a word," Newman told Félix in 2015. "I can't explain the feeling. At the moment I haven't gotten any endorsements or received any payment. I feel that I should be compensated. But I also feel that good things happen to those who wait."[10] Years after Louis C.K. donned a blaccent and called Leslie Jones's nails "on fleek" on the season finale of *Saturday Night Live*, Newman started a GoFundMe to raise money for a forthcoming line of hair and beauty products—only to be called entitled for the desire to profit from her own creation. In a 2017 interview with *Teen Vogue*, Newman admitted she would have been more proactive about retaining the term if she had known what the internet was going to do. On Fleek Extensions by Peaches Monroee launched that year. Newman told *The Fader*, "Now it's time for the world to get on fleek by me. Hahaha!"[11]

Vine was a white-hot sterling feature of a larger truth. The internet depends on black people.* Undeniable that so much content aggregated by millennial-targeted media orgs traces back to Black Tumblr, Black Twitter, and culture blogs. That research teams led by white faculty composed of white graduate students and maybe a token person of some color spend loads of time and grant money studying black internet communities. That so much language, fancifully attributed to internetspeak emerged from the diaspora online and off. That black language at large works as a sort of metastasized meme, replicated by entities who crave access to an elusive cool. That the sum of reaction images employed to express emotions in lieu of text confesses a preference for black individuals. That femme black

---

*In 2017 two white Temple University students, Adam Gasiewski and Emily Beck, self-published a book called *Milk and Vine: Inspirational Quotes from Classic Vines*. A threadbare parody of Rupi Kaur's successful collections, *Milk and Vine* turns catchphrases from popular vines, mostly from black Viners, into minimalist poems. In 2018 they published a sequel. Selling for $6 a pop, neither book credits the users who provided Gasiewski and Beck with poetry. Both have the audacity to include a copyright warning: "No portion of this book may be copied, retransmitted, reposted, duplicated, or otherwise used without the express written approval of the author."

people, otherwise superfluous to their white and nonblack counterparts, become *so necessary* when it's time to bring *attitude*. That Nene Leakes and Oprah Winfrey and Ms. Foxy and Prince and Jasmine Masters help the likes of Meghan McCain and scores of white gay men find *their inner diva*.

In his 2006 master's thesis, Joshua Lumpkin Green introduces the term "digital blackface" to describe how technology enables nonblack individuals to slip into black personhood.[12] Taking the game *Grand Theft Auto: San Andreas* as a case, Green argues that the medium "allows the player the avenue to safely experience the thrill of racialized violence and eroticized sex" though its black protagonist. Digital blackface extends the historical and ongoing minstrel practice that gives it its name, but new technology also "presents whole new type of animal, more dangerous and more pervasive" than anything before.[13] Adding to Green's work, art historian Kate Brown applies the concept of digital blackface to the prevalence of reaction gifs on Tumblr of black women and queer black men that often take on a "minstrelsy quality."[14] Animated gifs now function as forms of communication, Brown explains, and how we use them to express ourselves expresses something about how we see ourselves and want others to see us, our identity. "The images that inundate our online world have the potential to create virtual tourists."

In between these regular appropriations, swarms of card-carrying Nazis impersonate black identity behind fictitious profiles. Hailing from crude message boards, relics of an online beforetime, hoards of white people blacken up their social media profiles in order to infiltrate online discussions about justice. As they try on black vernacular language for size, their posts and tweets can read like corporate coolspeak, but motivated by chaos as much as greed. Their goal is to muss up whatever the topic is at hand. They are men, usually, but not always. Autonomy expressed by both people of color and white women has them fit to be tied and ready to harass. Years before Jack and Zuck and tech journalism, before the federal government, decided to investigate the alt-right trolls better called white supremacists, critics and thinkers like Anita Sarkeesian and Shafiqah Hudson and I'Nasah Crockett and Sydette Harry saw the terror behind the scenes, the frothing hatred of men so desperate to stymie equality that they'll willingly don masks (again).

In June 2014, Hudson uncovered an organized campaign called Operation: Lollipop. Started on 4chan, Operation: Lollipop gathered together men's rights and pickup artist enthusiasts and otherwise unaffiliated racists and misogynists. The campaign, which had been going on for at least a year, urged fanatics to "infiltrate feminists movements with twitter accounts and conduct a black propaganda campaign to secure classified objectives." By mimicking the social justice discourse that was by then thriving, Operation: Lollipop wanted to pit activists against each other. The idea was to drip the poison slowly, impersonate black and East Asian women and introduce enough disagreement to invite arguments, but not sound so off-base that genuine activists would consider it futile to engage. The idea was also to attract the attention of weaker allies, male feminists and white liberals, who but needed the slightest nudge to doubt the cause. (It is no fluke that they dressed up as women *of color*.) One account accumulated more than nine thousand followers before the jig was up.

Operation: Lollipop was revealed after #EndFathersDay and #WhitesCantBeRaped trended worldwide on Twitter the Friday before the holiday. By the weekend, Fox News host Tucker Carlson had worked up a lather over #EndFathersDay, and *Fox & Friends* invited the author Susan Patton onto the show to browbeat the alleged feminists responsible.* "They're not just interested in ending Father's Day. They're interested in ending men," said Patton. However, the "they" in this case would be the men behind Operation: Lollipop, whom Fox never identified. Instead, it was up to Hudson to create #YourSlipIsShowing, which began tracking suspicious activity from accounts run by people who weren't who they claimed to be. As Hudson and other contributors to the archive such as Crockett and Harry found, fake accounts have tells visible to those who pay attention. Observers can spot the ones who've amassed fluency in black vernacular and radical politics through cable television. Observers, however, must first be willing to give blackness and feminism the benefit

---

* If you are drawing a blank here, Patton is the self-described "Princeton Mom" who wrote an op-ed for the *Daily Princetonian* telling college women to focus on husband-hunting instead of their studies, advice she later spun into a book. Patton also appeared on CNN calling rape "not a crime," but "a learning experience" (see Susan Patton, " 'Marry Smart': 'Princeton Mom' Susan Patton's Manifesto for Domestic Bliss," *Today*, March 10, 2014).

of the doubt. Yet, there are as many fake allies as there are fake accounts. People believe the hoaxes they want to be true.

YourSlipIsShowing is ongoing because the campaigns are ongoing. With fascism at home in the White House, certain groups only grew emboldened online and off. The freedom afforded these men, the fluid, choose-for-yourself bodilessness special to the internet, was once so crucial to the many people for whom existing in the outside world incurs risk. Once havens of a sort, online platforms have become liabilities to the well-being of anyone not already fiercely protected by the administration.

The scale between meme culture and virtual tourism and misinformation campaigns is slipperier than users warrant. The mere mention of "digital blackface" prompts responses as interesting as the concept itself. There are the Good White People who stumble over each other to prove their goodness, who would declare the use of any gif verboten if a black person wished it so, but only if they could broadcast such on social media. This black person never asked for that, but Good White People don't care so much for reading and listening either, they want to fast-forward to whatever prescribed action alleviates their guilt. "The impulse towards action can work to block hearing," writes the feminist scholar Sara Ahmed. "In moving on from the present towards the future, it can also move away from the object of critique, or place the white subject 'outside' that critique in the present of the hearing."[15] It feels bad to wade in the repercussions of our behavior, it feels good to apologize and disavow and consider oneself exempt moving forward. But being online, being white, being online as a white person, means never being exempt. Antiracist as a noun does not exist. There's only people doing the work, or not. The person genuinely invested in the work doesn't run from discomfort but accepts it as the price of personhood taken for granted.

In terms of images, discomfort means knowing that circulation of any kind is never neutral. Even those willing to be convinced that blackness is both reviled and relied upon for what happens on the internet—an ambivalence to the tune of Eric Lott's classic study *Love and Theft*—tend to feel uneasy about the suggestion that the out-and-out racism of anonymous users bears any relation to their own, very casual, user behavior. But we all drink from the well poisoned by the anti-blackness that wants everyone to forget when blackness goes viral.

The story tech tells is empty and incomplete. While that industry entertains itself with a fantasy of how the internet came to be, the truth throbs in the living tissue of our interfaces. Whether black people will be acknowledged and allowed to thrive more than spiritually from their innovations remains to be seen. Silicon Valley can ignore every sign of life on this planet, but will never escape the blackness of the web.

CHAPTER 6

The Viral Star

Opposite from Stardom

They would applaud his courage while they stretched his neck.

Homelessness is a crisis that, if you're lucky, never happens to you. Many, however, live in a suspended state of perpetually tenuous living called houselessness. Houselessness is denoted not so much as a lack of roof over one's head but rather looks like the problem of too many roofs. House-lessness means a vulnerable position that's also invisible: the roof or sublet or room or couch or *yeah, sure, just crash here for the weekend* is a mask that keeps concern at bay. Strangers, employers, even relatives are short on empathy for those who they assume are at least meeting the physiologi-cal minimums in the famed hierarchy of needs. As a society we are bad enough to people who certainly aren't. It isn't a competition to be sure, for houselessness makes a poor consolation prize, more a transient condi-tion punctuated by periods of homelessness, stability, houselessness, and back again. A delayed check, closed office, changed schedule, misread ad-dress, an administrative shutdown, an overlooked e-mail—the frustrated reminders that slow still exists in a world where messages cross the ocean in less than a breath—might mean the difference between living or not. This is the usual.

And, then, sometimes the circumstances that tip the scale are more divinely wrought: sometimes crisis begins in fire.

On April 7, 2012, a fire broke out in an apartment complex in the Pennville neighborhood of Oklahoma City, Oklahoma. Though no serious injuries were reported, one woman—in whose home the fire started—was treated for smoke inhalation and five units were damaged, displacing several families and depriving many more of electricity. KFOR-TV, an NBC affiliate, reported the story, which included a brief interview with one of the residents, Kimberly Wilkins, who ran for her life as the building burned.[1]

On camera, the light is enough to make out the smoke-stained wall behind her, yet it's unclear how much time separates the witness exclusive from the event witnessed. Wilkins, shot from the shoulders up, her head nearly filling the frame, appears on camera with all the warmth of a ghost—ashy, as someone less sympathetic might say—whether washed by fear, stress, or the spotlight it's also hard to tell. The pixie cut mostly hidden in a neatly knotted scarf might be wrapped for bed or ready for some fifteen seconds of fame.

Watching Wilkins I am reminded of those unfortunate souls on *The Bachelor*, or any other show where personalities are made from a single serendipitous sound bite. I remember learning how contestants are manipulated into showing their worst selves, kept awake at ungodly hours and plied with many, many glasses of whatever libations ABC is willing to pay for. What does it feel like to be on camera at your most vulnerable, whether intoxicated, tired, or really, really scared? Reporters have a habit of following black people at our most exhausted moments—sports media, for one, depends on it. It's funny when these subjects garble overwrought platitudes like "win some, lose some," as if anybody else could do better when mic'd up for the whole world to hear after sprinting for four quarters in an arena temperature controlled for the comfort of spectators, not their entertainment. It's amazing that the words come at all.

Of course, these and other considerations are considerations only available in retrospect. Recorded live in the moment nobody has the time. On April 7, 2012, a fire broke out, a woman was unhomed, and, camera on, the words came. On April 7, 2012, a fire broke out and Kimberly Wilkins, newly homeless, spilled out the words that forever immortalized her as Sweet Brown, viral video star: "Lord Jesus there's a fire."

During the rise of Sweet Brown, I laughed with everyone else. I laughed at the ashen mouth with lips split a thousand ways. I laughed at the scarf. I laughed at the various songs that appeared on YouTube, Brown's voice chopped, auto tuned, and remixed over electro rhythms as is customary. I laughed until I heard "ain't nobody got time for that" in the mouth of a tiny speck of a white girl, and then suddenly I wasn't laughing and she wasn't laughing but she still was in a way. I wasn't laughing; I was sick.

In 2008, Diane Lane starred in *Untraceable*, a movie about a Saw-type serial killer who streams the deaths of his victims live at the slippery false-front website KillWithMe.com. As the URL suggests, users who visit the website become implicated in fatal torture; the intensity of method, and subsequently pace of death, is directly proportional to the site's hit counter. Lane plays an FBI special agent (naturally) named Jennifer Marsh who makes the killer her single-minded mission (naturally), working alongside Colin Hanks aka Agent Griffin Dowd. (He eventually bites the dust when submerged in a bathtub filled with an increasingly concentrated solution of sulfuric acid.)

Untraceable was too bad to be taken seriously and too committed to gore porn per genre standard to make for an honest satire of the practice it also revels in. It was also too predictive to be of its time. Lane's antagonist is ultimately revealed to be a tech prodigy, while her nemesis throughout the film is really tech itself. Before Periscope, before Snapchat, when Twitter was just one and a half years old and live video was only tentatively so, *Untraceable* imagined an internet where the bandwidth for death is endlessly expandable and servers are immortal, even if we aren't.

But it was 2008. Few wanted to believe tech was the enemy in 2008. Few wanted to believe that that world was our world. "Morally duplicitous torture porn," the *New York Times* called it; "sleazy and gratuitous," said *USA Today*.[2] One critic at the *Apollo Guide* waited a whole year and a half to call the movie "prototype Internet conspiracy drivel."[3] Altogether, consensus rendered the film's plot a too-convenient bit o' techno imagineering for an ultimate pursuit of gore and bits, as contrived as the instruments of death themselves. They were halfway correct. The internet that *Untraceable* envisions exists—the movie was technically accurate—but its victims do not. *Untraceable* is far too white to pass for reality. White death may be sensational, but never goes viral.

Viral video was once a much tamer thought, populated by cute baby Brits named Charlie, doped up unicorns (also named Charlie), and rock bands on treadmills. Nobody feared "going viral" because going viral, far from having any sinister connotation, was the goal. We can't hope to fathom the storage space remaining to this day reserved for the preservation of all the foregone viral wannabes—a regular island of misfit megabytes still searching for their fifteen minutes of "Keyboard Cat" fame. You can't blame anyone for having tried. This was a golden era, where a working webcam might land you a spot on *Good Morning America* and from there the world was yours, provided you could monetize this newfound relevance faster than public's capacity to forget. This was before "trending," or maybe back when trending rather meant the beginning of something, not someone's end.

Blackness gave virality its teeth. Turned it into trauma. Cops killing black people is too traditional, too historical, too common, so that it's not only cliché but writing about it has become so. Newspapers and magazines only, and still reluctantly, cover black death when the buzz borders on frenzy—not because it happened but because it went viral. The media sits and waits for a name to trend that doesn't belong to a (yet) public figure. Then they make them public. They trot out their Negro writer du jour and the Negro writer produces an aching tribute to being black in America. And another. And another. Et cetera.

I don't watch the videos. I can't and never will.

The cliché is so maybe because it seems cliché to remind everyone of something so cemented, so much in fact that even academia marks its evidence. "Race-based stress and trauma" is now a concept safe enough for *Psychology Today* to put on glossy paper, for a book of poetry, *Citizen: An American Lyric*, to be nominated and robbed, for an album, *Lemonade*, to be nominated and robbed, for *Between the World and Me* to be nominated and win. We know enough what video of this kind does to living black people, what it actuates and what it signifies. What it says about us. Watched or unwatched, black people are over and again witnesses to an event that forms the horizon of our existence. That's who we are, who we become.

We repeat this and we repeat repeating this and marking the repeating in words and data and poetry and find ourselves as we know ourselves to be. We know what going viral says about us. But what about everyone else?

If someone consumes anything at the pace and frequency that the internet consumes trauma with black subjects, we say something is wrong, that they have a problem. Drugs, hoarding, furries, video games, whatever, the new millennium has invented a myriad of resources to help a person and their loved ones deal with newfound obsessions enabled by the internet age. It seems we only don't consider gluttony a social sin if the thing gorged on is a black person in distress. In that case, the gratuitous replays and retweets aren't disordered, just the internet as usual. Topless women and bare asses get deleted from most social media platforms, but videos of black people in trouble are left untouched. Google Search won't recognize the word "blow job," but type in Philando Castile's and Jazmine Headley's names and the engine autofills an invitation to the abuse.

America is addicted to hurting black people. America is addicted to watching itself hurt black people. The internet didn't invent this kind of spectacle, nor is it the source of the disease, but rather collaborates with the country's disregard for the black lives without which it wouldn't exist. Black people taught the internet how to go viral. But when virality became enterprise, black people were seldom to be found.

Logan Paul has over twenty-one million subscribers on YouTube. He is in his early twenties and part of the class of online stars called YouTubers. He, as does his younger brother Jake, uploads near daily video blogs along with short comedic skits and musical numbers. In a video called "No Handlebars," the blond, blue-eyed, denim-clad twenty-two-year-old delivers rudimentary rhymes over a trapified interpolation of the alt-hop group Flobots' 2008 single "Handlebars." He brags about his ability to have sex with another man's woman "with no handlebars" as per the chorus. The video has over forty-one million views. In another video, *Kong Killed Another Animal . . .*, Paul talks to the camera while he brings a small dog outside to frolic in the snow, drives around with his brother, and encounters fans who've brought him dinner plates, an in-joke referencing a running gag in Paul's videos where he smashes a plate on the floor in front of his assistant, Ayla, a fellow YouTuber.[4] This is a job. Forbes once estimated Paul's yearly earnings at $12.5 million, slightly ahead of his brother's $11.5 million.[5] Apart from millions made on YouTube through high view counts on videos monetized through ad revenue, Paul can earn around $100,000 per Facebook or Instagram post and has been sponsored by HBO, Nike, Verizon, and Pepsi.

I was introduced to Logan's work at the nail salon when the owner gave her pint-sized relative control over the large smart TV mounted in the back corner. By her deft selection, the room was dragged into the wild world of YouTube's elite, a colorful, high-energy, pitched-up world that made me feel ancient, although the performers and I are basically the same age. I had heard of Logan only briefly before as the subject of a trending controversy a few months prior. Early in 2018, Logan vlogged his walk through Japan's Aokigahara forest—a common site for suicides—including the moment he and his friends encountered the body of a person who died by apparent suicide. Though his posse cut the excursion short and contacted authorities, Logan still posted the video, which swiftly attracted attention well beyond his regular viewership. He took a compulsory hiatus, ending a streak of daily uploads lasting from September 12, 2016, to January 1, 2018. He returned a month later, reaping millions of views on videos such as *We Rescued a Baby Duckling!* and *Releasing My $10,000 Albino Turtle!*[6]

As I learned that day in the salon, Logan is not a fluke in the system by any means. Though he lives closer to the top of the mountain than most, he merely represents an echelon of YouTubers who are all striving for the same thing. Some are more inclined to pranks, some play video games, some do makeup or orchestrate elaborate DIY crafts, some film heavily choreographed videos on soundstages for audibly auto-tuned songs that sound like they come from a twenty-five-cent candy dispenser. All are reaching for something more precious than gold: attention. They are a long way from their predecessors, more like sophisticated fracking rigs compared to pioneering viral sensations who landed on fame by accident. In a booming market with not enough eyes and ears to go around, they're vying for a mere fraction of what Kimberly Wilkins struck simply fleeing for her life while a building burned. Unlike Wilkins, though, some from this new breed of internet sensations see themselves paid handsomely for the trouble.

In the race to figure out just how to make a buck or two or millions from social media stardom, there was never going to be room for everybody. While time and attention seem like limitless quantities when it comes to teens and young adults, they, too, only have twenty-four hours a day and more responsibility to manage that time wisely than any other generation in history. YouTubers are well aware that they need to reel audiences in fast and for good—as are advertisers. In the world of YouTube, money has a way of stratifying things, putting premiums on some content over others. Without it, the playing field would be more level, giving at least the appearance that anyone might get lucky enough to strike a following. YouTube was once this way. Vine, too, while it lasted. When Vine was shut down by Twitter precisely because it didn't want to make its platform more amenable to creators getting paid, many viral sensations on that app, many young and black, lost their audiences in an instant.

Companies of all kinds eventually learned how to employ YouTube sensations to the best advantage, not just through the ads we sit through but through coveted real estate in the mouths of the YouTubers themselves, delivered straight to viewers who would take years to develop discernment for that type of thing. When the money got involved, it had that way of doing what money always does, following the path of least resistance en route to more money, more capital. Like Logan spitting bars on a bike in a Canadian tuxedo, many of the most famous YouTube celebrities are very, very white. White and light faces are the safest gamble, the money decided, better yet if they can fashion a creole persona—black aesthetics on a visage that's anything but. It's a reciprocal relationship, though advertisers hold the power. YouTubers get an influx of funds to pay for studio time, better equipment, or rent. Companies get a roster of pale to spray-tanned beauty gurus, for example, who speak a snappy *heygirlheyohsnapslaytreatyoself!* dialect learned from hours of internet use and NBC programming. Or, maybe just wiggers like the Pauls, or gamers and comics who do nothing but be safely not black. It's not guaranteed insurance. In 2017, user PewDiePie—93 million subscribers and counting—whose real name is Felix Kjellberg, called someone a "fucking nigger" during a livestream. This was months after Disney and YouTube Red, YouTube's subscription streaming service, severed ties with Kjellberg for paying two Indian freelancers on Fiverr to write "Death to all Jews" on camera. (It was not his first dip into anti-Semitism.) And shortly after Logan received scrutiny for his Aokigahara forest video, video of Jake surfaced on *TMZ* showing the slightly less popular Paul freestyling about "little-ass niggas." Jeffree Star (fourteen million), Tana Mongeau (three million), and Kathleen Lights (four million), influencers from the glam corner of the 'Tube have each been caught saying the N-word at least once. The counterbalance to virality is stardom.

Like the old Negro adage, being black on YouTube means being caught in the mire of twice as good, half as much. Only maybe more like ten times as good for a tenth of the glory and financial security, growing worse as the platform becomes more saturated. The more YouTube wants to resemble traditional mass media, the more old media rules define new media venues. For every Kingsley and Franchesca Ramsey, for every hilarious black person who's found shine after toiling on YouTube for over a decade, there are thousands of mediocre white talents fast-tracked to relevance. And to make the leap from YouTube to the more traditional, more solid, better-paying gigs, the work must be the best of the best—akin to Issa Rae or Donald Glover.

I am at this very moment transfixed by a YouTube channel belonging to someone named Jay Nedaj. Nedaj writes, directs, stars in, and edits an offbeat novella set on a plantation called *Word on the Crops: If Slaves Had a Reality TV Show*. The name itself is a riot, relocating "word on the street" to the cash-crop fields, an irreverent calling back that defines the terms of the show. In the opening sequence Nedaj walks in slow motion down a suburban deck, which here functions as a sweeping Southern veranda. Here he plays the role of Carla, wearing a sweater, an apron, and a long brown skirt. He keeps his facial hair, mustache, and goatee. Carla twirls in slow motion while the show theme plays, a work song sung by Ed Lewis and recorded by Alan Lomax in the thirties. "I'll be so glad (uh huh) when the sun goes down (when the sun goes down). I'll be so glad (uh huh) when the sun goes down (when the sun goes down)." The show's fifth episode begins with Carla in prayer. "Dear God, or whoever you are, why are you doing this to me? I'm trying to believe in you. But it's hard." There's a low, rhythmic hum in the background. The show whips into a musical number: set to "Brown Betty" from a 2015 Broadway cast recording of the musical *The Color Purple*. I've never seen anything like it. (Tarantino *wishes*.) Nedaj's following, presently under one hundred thousand subscribers, is modest by YouTube standards. If Nedaj were white, the next season of *Word on the Crops* would surely be slated to appear on Netflix already. Perhaps an exaggeration. Perhaps not.

Elsewhere, it is not so hard for black people to bring in viewers. Just die and die spectacularly at the hands of the state. Don't rely on the officer's dash- or bodycam, though; those have a tendency to skip ahead or go dark at the most inopportune moments and then your death will have been in vain—and no, no one will care about some witness's elaborate statement if the office can show a ruddy bruise on his upper cheek. Make sure there is a cameraman. Make sure they have a Twitter account. Make sure they have several, for when the first account is suspended for anti-cop hate speech. Make sure they know the consequences. They will likely be the only one serving time when' all is said and done.

Going viral sounds like immortality, but it is ultimately the user who craves it. It's a short trip to turn black people into bits. Images, mannerisms, language captured forever in looping GIFs and autoplay, cycling at inhumane speeds long after lips have stopped moving. It can only be by design that we are uniquely lubricated for the tubules that make up the networks that spider across borders, under oceans, into space, into homes, into hands. We live and die by the internet. The internet asks for more.

PART IV

Economy and Politics

CHAPTER 7

The Chef

America's Whiteface Mammy

And yet not all her reverence for her old mistress, nor all her deference to the whites, nor all their friendship for her, had been able to save her from this raging devil of race hatred which momentarily possessed the town.

There's a version of this story that starts with slavery. It starts on the plantation in the Big House, where missus and master and chirren sit to feast on the sweat, grease, blood, tears, and shit that goes into some real down-home country cooking before there was such a phrase, back when it was just called supper. Or maybe it starts earlier, behind the Big House, in the tucked-away second building where the real business of shucking, slicing, seasoning, mixing, boiling, firing, and cooking got down.[1] The building constructed by, in author Charles W. Chesnutt's imagination, the transfigured body of a runaway slave who whispered with his lover at night. Maybe it begins with the slaughter or in the smokehouse. Maybe it begins in the gardens and the fields, where green thumbs and agrarian know-how coaxed heirloom plants to life. Maybe it begins with another kind of slaughter, at Manifest Destiny, that genocidal regime which took and took and took, including the farming and cooking techniques of Native peoples. Maybe it begins at the cusp, that serendipitous between time when Europeans hadn't yet unleashed full devastation (as far as North America was concerned), when multicultural—in a truer sense than we know it today—communities of Native, African, and European couldn't

help but absorb one another's lessons for living. But it could also begin
earlier, on the moaning ship, in the barracoon, back to a third kind of
slaughter. There's a version of this story that starts with murder, kidnapping, genocide. There's a version that starts before all that, the prelapsarian
moment when what's now called Africa was allowed to be cosmopolitan
without prejudice. But I want to start with Paula.

America loves Paula Deen.

Her story starts with overcoming. Paula had a "delicious childhood,"
per her memoir, growing up in Albany, Georgia.[2] By young adulthood,
however, her life felt dire. "The tragedies began," she writes. "And with
them, I began to die." By twenty-three Deen lost both her parents to
repeated health problems, and she was left with "a sour marriage" (to
an abusive alcoholic), two young children, her sixteen-year-old younger
brother, and a creeping anxiety of the outside world. "I started waking
up many mornings and wondering if this was the day I'd die," said Paula.
"And these thoughts just went on and on for twenty years, more or less."
In the decades spent mostly confined to her home due to severe agoraphobia, she perfected recipes passed down from her grandmomma Paul:
turtle soup, fried chicken, and fried peach pies; dishes seasoned with herbs,
fatback, peppers, and hog jowls. Too poor for therapy and unsupported
by her faith, it wasn't until her divorce in her forties that Paula returned
to the world, selling bagged lunches filled with ham and chicken salad
sandwiches and banana pudding to workers in downtown Savannah. She
opened a small restaurant, then another, bigger restaurant. She published a
cookbook with Random House in 1998; it was featured by QVC and sold
seventy thousand copies in one day.* Within five years she would make
appearances on *The Oprah Winfrey Show* and host her own show, *Paula's
Home Cooking,* on the Food Network. Within another five years she would

---

*The year 1998 was also when the soul food legend Princess Pamela Strobel closed her
popular East Village establishment in New York City and virtually disappeared from the
face of the earth. Princess Pamela was effectively forgotten to the annals of American cuisine until Matt and Ted Lee found her 1969 cookbook of 147 recipes, *Princess Pamela's Soul
Food Cookbook,* in a used-book store in 2004. It returned to print in 2017. Food and culture
writer Mayukh Sen, who won a James Beard award in 2018 for his profile of Pamela in
Food52, writes that our threadbare notice of someone like Strobel is "indicative of a greater
systemic ill that plagues America's culinary memory."

boast of having two restaurants, a magazine, several television shows, numerous cookbooks, her own line of cook stuffs, and a minor role in the 2005 film *Elizabethtown*.

Paula became the face of Southern cuisine, though the better qualifier for her dishes is more like "comfort food." Baked macaroni and cheese, creamy mashed potatoes, cheesy grits, fried chicken, mayo-forward slaws, peach cobbler à la mode, peanut butter balls, a burger sandwiched between two doughnuts—her recipes don't summon a particularly vivid sense of any region that calls itself Southern. They do evoke a cadre of emotions that non-Southerners like to pin on the South: warmth, simplicity, nostalgia, and, again, comfort. It's the kind of food ordained to precede a nap, that fitness fanatics avoid like the plague or maybe reserve for the ill-fated "cheat day." Butter, lots of it, mayonnaise by the tub, fat-soaked vegetables, cheddar oozing everywhere, liberal salt and pepper, but spices on the sparse side. Paula's critics call her a "convenience cook," a label shared with the Food Network talent Rachael Ray, denoting cooks who are more personality than chef. If true, convenience, like comfort, is still a virtue to the Southern nonchef. Cutting cheesecake slices to be covered in chocolate, rolled into wonton wrappers, deep-fried, and doused with powdered sugar, Paula permits viewers to start with something from the frozen food section or "You can make your own," she says offhand with no further instructions on how that might be done. Her "Symphony Brownies" begin with prepackaged brownie mix; the "special" twist is a layer of Hershey's chocolate bars inside the batter. No harried parent or broke college student or first-time dinner host will encounter a fatiguing list of ingredients when they turn to one of Paula's recipes. Paula's recipe for fried chicken only requires three seasonings: salt, black pepper, and garlic powder.

Then there is the woman herself. She's straight from a Disney picture—and not *Song of the South*, but something more Renaissance era, when stereotypes were still fun and racism much less obvious, even if the back of your mind knew it was there. She's the grandmother urbane Yankees try to forget and feel tremendously guilty about, for which they must find an appropriate surrogate. She's not perfect or polished; she licks her thumb and covers imperfections with fudge and confectioner's sugar. She'll gasp upon seeing a gooey trail of melted cheese and treat a burger with a fried egg on top like a Travel Channel–worthy adventure—and she likes that burger *medium well*. She's stout like people say they like their cooks (even if female chefs—celebrity or otherwise—rarely escape size-based scrutiny). She's safe in the way America desexualizes women of her age and size, and yet she gets to be forever girlish. In short, she's white Mammy, plumping America one fried delicacy at a time.

In March 2012, Lisa Jackson, the white former manager of Uncle Bubba's Seafood & Oyster House, in Savannah, Georgia, filed a lawsuit against the owners, Deen and her brother (Bubba Deen) on the grounds of racism and sexual harassment. Jackson claimed that black employees were held to a higher standard of performance and required to use bathrooms and entrances separate from white employees. She also alleged that Bubba often made racist remarks and sexual comments and forced her to look at pornography with him in addition to putting his hands on other employees. Paula was accused of enabling her brother's behavior. Worse, the suit describes Paula's involvement in Bubba's 2007 wedding as an out-and-out desire to fully re-create an Old South fantasy, with Negro tap dancers and all. In May 2013, Paula gave a videotaped deposition and in June 2013, *National Enquirer* claimed it had the footage. Within twenty-four hours the transcript of that deposition showed up online. Paula denied the discrimination allegations against her and her brother, but what she did reveal was almost as bad. She admitted to expressing her hope that her brother would experience a genuine Southern plantation wedding reminiscent of an antebellum or postbellum era when black people waited on white people. She admitted to living in a household where jokes involving the N-word are told to her "constantly."[3] When asked if she had ever used the N-word herself, Paula responded, "Yes, of course."[4]

It was the N-word heard around the world—*again*—and she hadn't even said it on camera. That latter detail offered just the wiggle room needed to turn Paula into the subject of debate. The suit was dismissed without award in August 2013, but Food Network, Walmart, Target, Sears, Kmart, Home Depot, Walgreens, and several other companies had already cut ties with Paula over a month earlier. Other former employees came forward with allegations against Paula and Bubba—including one who said they were repeatedly called "my little monkey"—but the loss of Paula's bread and butter was all that was needed to martyr her. While the nation had one dry eye trained on the trial and acquittal of the man who killed a young black teen in cold blood, its other eye teared up for Paula, who released not one but two videos apologizing "to everybody. For the wrong that I've done." CNN solicited fellow Georgia native Jimmy Carter to weigh in, who felt perhaps the hammer was brought down too harshly. Sales of Paula's most recent cookbook soared, jumping from the 1,500s to the number one spot in Amazon sales.

Paula did not go gently into that good night, and to those ignorant of the scandal it might look like she was having her best years ever. She raised at least $75 million for her company Paula Deen Ventures from a private investment firm.[5] She bought the rights to her Food Network shows and began streaming them on the Paula Deen Network, her own subscription streaming platform. She appeared on Matt Lauer's *Today* show with her sons Jamie and Bobby to tout her new enterprise—and also sorta reflect on the fallout from the deposition. She appeared on *Steve Harvey*, again with Jamie and Bobby in tow, to do the same. She joined ABC's *Dancing with the Stars* and made it to week six, when she was eliminated for a dry re-creation of Madonna's mesmerizing "Vogue" performance at the 1990 MTV Video Music Awards. She opened a cookware store. She went on a twenty-city Paula Deen Live! tour. She reissued her own out-of-print cookbooks. She opened new restaurants under the Paula Deen's Family Kitchen franchise, promising "a family-style dining experience born from the classic recipes of the Queen of Southern Cuisine herself."[6] She launched a clothing line with a creative name—Paula Deen's Closet. Jamie and Bobby got their own Food Network show called *Southern Fried Road Trip*.

It's amazing what America finds room to forgive and what it has no room for. N-word-gate was not Paula's first controversy. In 2012, she had visited the *Today* show to announce that she had been diagnosed with type-2 diabetes and had been knowingly living with it for three years. She also announced, in nearly the same breath, her partnership with Nova Nordisk, a Danish pharmaceutical company that sells the diabetes drug Victoza. The bald-faced doubled-up announcement confirmed everything her eagle-eyed critics knew to be true. Months prior to her announcement, the late Anthony Bourdain said, in an interview with *TV Guide*, "The worst, most dangerous person to America is clearly Paula Deen. She revels in unholy connections with evil corporations and she's proud of the fact that her food is f—ing bad for you."* He added, "Plus, her food sucks."[7] Hounded for a follow-up quote after rumors of Paula's impending diabetes news came to light, Bourdain had his own question: "How long has she known?"

People felt hoodwinked. There seemed to be something profoundly wrong with using a platform to push buttery, sugary, mayo-laden meals while treating a condition with causal relation in popular culture, if not quite in medicine, to those ingredients. It didn't make the most sense— bacon-wrapped fried mac and cheese doesn't develop a complex nutrient profile if the person cooking it *doesn't* have diabetes. But people thought Paula had been irresponsible and was now trying to profit from the anti- dote to her "bad" behavior. She'd eventually put out a new *New York Times* bestseller, *Paula Deen Cuts the Fat*. Bobby Deen got his own spin-off brand, debuting his show the same year called *Not My Mama's Meals*, remaking "classic" Paula recipes with less fat and calories. The jig was too transparent.

Americans felt more affronted and returned more cruelty when they decided the woman had gotten ill from her own supply than when they discovered she was probably racist. Making us fat was unforgivable, but the N-word was a gray area. I believe Ms. Deen could have walked right up to the camera and flipped the bird with a hearty "Fuck you, nigger!" and still be forgiven by white America and Steve Harvey. Her easy journey back into our good graces says as much.

The problem with Paula actually has little to do with whether or not she's racist. It's not so much a matter of the aftermath, but of how a woman like Paula got to be Paula in the first place. Why was Paula Deen, whose coherent Southern-isms boil down to an accent, a tan, and a countri- fied kitchen, allowed to be *the* singular word on Southern cooking for over a decade? There are absolutely country people—which includes the

---

*Bourdain later corrected *TV Guide*'s transcript via tweet: "My comment was actually 'worst, most dangerous to America cook on FN [Food Network].'"

North- and Southwest, Midwest, and East and West Coasts—like Paula who cook with Fritos and Bisquick and make do with packaged staples in trying to stretch a dollar in an unforgiving economy. But that's not why people loved Paula. Deen amassed an empire because she represented the version of Southern culture American morality wanted to live with. The recipes not attributed to her innate Southern instincts have been vaguely passed down by some ur-Southern relative, neatly side-stepping any reasonable query into when a black person factors into that inheritance—and in the South, it *is* a matter of when, not if.

In Paula's case we needn't search for long. Dora Charles, a Savannah-based black chef descended from Lowcountry sharecroppers, was the unsung backbone of Paula's enterprises. She opened Paula and Bubba's Lady & Sons alongside the pair, though not as co-owner, but by developing recipes and training cooks on a wage of less than ten dollars an hour, she told the *New York Times* in 2013.[8] This did not change when Paula made it to television. "It's just time that everybody knows that Paula Deen don't treat me the way they think she treat me," she said, adding more support to circulating claims that Paula's N-word use wasn't a one-time far-off affair but part of her everyday speech.[9] Before things took off, Paula made Charles a promise: "Stick with me, Dora, and I promise you one day if I get rich you'll get rich."[10] But once the riches came, Paula wasn't sharing. Not until 2015 would Charles have the opportunity to publish her own book with a major publisher after decades of hustling in Paula's shadow.*

Paula, still wealthy, now moves mostly in the background, letting major distributors, syndication, and royalties do the work. Since the height of her visibility, a craft revolution has changed the public's relationship to the things people put in their mouths, or at least their ideas about their relationship to the things they put in their mouths. People now want small-batch beer and ancient-grain bread, artisanal ice cream and old-school butchers and mayonnaise made from non-GMO oils and eggs laid by free-roaming chickens. Those who can afford to wave away the processed and mass-produced have done so in search of something *authentic.* This

---

*Charles is literally out of focus, standing behind Paula's left shoulder, on the cover of the 2013 cookbook *Paula Deen & Friends: Living It Up, Southern Style.*

includes a more rigorous interest in genuine Southern cooking in the most varied sense: regional BBQ, Lowcountry boils, backwoods moonshine, freshwater fish fry. But if America has learned anything from its love affair with Paula, that wisdom remains to be seen. The who's who lists of heritage cooking are largely white. Even the resurgence of barbeque, possibly the blackest cooking technique within US borders, jushed and priced up to befit artisanal obsessions, is being led by mostly white pitmasters. Zagat's "12 Pitmasters You Need to Know Around the U.S." mentions only two black pitmasters, Ed Mitchell and Rodney Scott. Mitchell and Scott, each extraordinary, are customarily the lone black folks on such lists. (A 2015 Fox News compilation of "America's most influential BBQ pitmasters and personalities" managed to avoid black people altogether.)

Instead of reckoning with Southern food's past (and present), white Americans fuss over the small, monied group of restaurateurs who may brand themselves hands-on archivists; it is another form of fetishism, another way for liberal white Americans to have the South they want (pleasant, rich, storied, flavorful) without the black and brown people who remind them of how the South came to be the South. On the Netflix series *Ugly Delicious*, charismatic chef and author David Chang puts that erasure front and center in an episode on fried chicken, which has also experienced a cultural renaissance under the guidance of white hipster chefs. Across the series Chang is often interested in where singularity meets reality and the frankly delicious mess that immigration, migration, globalization, and commercialization have made of any idea of a "pure" food culture. He travels to Tokyo, where esteemed chef Zaiyu Hasegawa's fried chicken adaptations start with KFC as the holy grail, seemingly extricated from the historical burden embedded in the same dish in the United States; Chang sits at the kitchen counter of Atlanta-based chef and author Asha Gomez, whose fried chicken people attribute to a "Southern American" influence but is actually inspired by her South Indian roots in Kerala. "I have to let them know," she tells Chang alongside writer and filmmaker Lois Eric Ellie, "that *every* culture figured out if you drenched a bird in flour and deep fried it, it was probably gonna be good."[11] Chang asks to taste her marinade, shifting raw chicken aside. His eyes widen. "That almost tastes like kimchi to me."

Chang is also cognizant that sometimes, and perhaps even most often, the liveliest developments in food culture come from the people descended from the ones who started it—whether "it" is kimchi or fried chicken. He visits the black-owned Bolton's Spicy Chicken & Fish in Nashville, whose Dollye Graham-Matthews proudly claims Bolton's as "the ones who put [hot chicken] on the map."* He also visits the white-owned Hattie B's Hot Chicken, opened in 2012, which has swept the hearts and press of audiences well outside Nashville. In 2016, *Food Republic*'s George Embiricos credited Hattie B's white executive chef John Lasater with putting hot chicken on the map. "Prince's Hot Chicken Shack may have created hot chicken in the 1930s, and institutions like Bolton's Spicy Chicken & Fish may have helped preserve the tradition over the years, but Hattie B's has made hot chicken cool," wrote Embiricos, consciously brushing aside nearly a century of black history.[12]

Sitting with Chang and the white Southern chef Sean Brock, Hattie B's co-owner Nick Jr. Bishop explains that his dad, owner of a suburban meat and three, would frequent chicken spots like Prince's and Bolton's. The two began experimenting with their own version of hot chicken, started selling it, and eventually founded Hattie B's out of love for the idiosyncratically Nashville product. Chang doesn't beat around the bush. "Are you aware of what critics say about you guys?" Bishop hems and stalls. Chang asks another, much more difficult question. "How do you be respectful?" Bishop looks at a loss, hard-pressed to answer the question that in truth has no answer that would allow him to continue restauranting with a clear conscience. "I can't tackle all of the bigger stuff by myself," Bishop responds. "I just know that as long as we're good sort of tenants of it, um, that's the best we can do. I'll always pay an homage to the Prince's and being able to tell that story of Bolton's, and the people

---

* The matter of who made hot chicken famous is, unsurprisingly, disputed. A Tennessee-based scholar, Rachel Louise Martin, and the editor in chief of the *Advocate* magazine, Zach Stafford, have written fascinating and exhaustive dives into hot chicken's trajectory in food culture: "How Hot Chicken Really Happened" in *The Bitter Southerner* and "Burned Out" in *Eater*. Both credit Prince's BBQ Chicken Shack as the one that started it all, though whether that's the same as putting it on the map is, I suppose, subjective. The James Beard Foundation has given Ms. André, the owner of Prince's Hot Chicken Shack, an America's Classics award for founding the regional and now national dish.

that paved the way before we ever were even thought of." Chang presses, posing a hypothetical that isn't so hypothetical in properly urban centers where trendy fusion cuisine steadily pushes less decorated ethnic options to the margins: "But what if you start killing the very thing that inspired this?" Brock cuts in while Bishop watches thoughtfully. "When we take it on as our obsession and passion, there's a lot of stuff that comes along with that. There's a lot of stuff that comes along with that. And that's a lot more complex than just cooking food." As Bishop quickly adds, "Stuff that on the front end, you would have never thought about, 'cause you just wanted to make good food, right?"

The conversation doesn't go far in terms of geopolitical discourse, but Bishop stumbles on an insight. Most white chefs need never consider the racial and cultural implications of the food they make. To them, ingredients are just ingredients and techniques just techniques, there to be picked up and implemented and adjusted at will. Culture only comes in when it's time to give the dish a name, make it legible to broader audiences. They can take for granted that their food, no matter what tradition it's drawn from, what genre it fits into, will be given the benefit of the doubt of a fine food worth its price. Meanwhile certain *ethnic* food is presumed to be crude, artery-clogging, less sanitary, and produced by low-skilled workers, and therefore ought to be as cheap as possible.* Americans want their nine-dollar Chinese takeout and two-dollar tacos and chicken by the bucket, but they will pay premium prices if these dishes have the good fortune to be *elevated* by someone white and usually male. The same source of freedom for chefs of color is a crucible.

Chang understands. Kimchi and Korean food more broadly got picked up by the same wave that's seen white chefs discovering what non-European food traditions can do. "I see a lot of white guys making Korean food, and I'll be honest, it pisses the shit out of me, because

---

*As has also occurred with Mexican and Chinese foods, companies appropriate and mass-produce soul food and serve it up sans context, leading white people to conflate black celebratory dishes such as fried chicken and macaroni and cheese with everyday black cooking. In a June 6, 2014, *Slate* article titled "Gastronomic Bigotry," Andrew Simmons observed that Angelenos are more likely to accuse Asian and Latinx restaurants of giving them food poisoning.

it's everywhere now: kimchi this, kimchi that," he says to a round table with Eric Elie, showrunner David Simon (*The Wire*, *Treme*, *The Deuce*), and chef Nina Compton. "I'm like, 'You weren't ostracized in elementary school because everyone thought, when they visited your house, it smelled like garbage.' They didn't have to endure emotional hardship, and now it's cool." Journalist Serena Dai observes something similar in an article in *Eater* called "Please Stop Writing Racist Restaurant Reviews," written as a response to a review that rated a Chinese restaurant favorably because its owners are a "pair of non-Chinese Chinese food enthusiasts."[13] Andrew Steinthal, of the review site The Infatuation, called Chinese food "an exercise in extremism," ticking off stereotype after harmful stereotype about the range of fare one can find in New York City. "Stereotypes and misperceptions about food matter," writes Dai, "because distaste for a people's food is a tangible way to express distaste for the people themselves."[14] The same white Americans who jeer at the unfamiliar as their parents taught them to do, grow up, develop a food palate worth a damn, and decide all is well. When Secretary of Homeland Security Kirstjen Nielsen decided to dine at a Mexican restaurant the day beginning the Trump administration's all-out assault on the lives of immigrants, it is crucial that she dined at MXDC Cocina Mexicana, owned by prolific restaurateur Todd English, which "offers classic Mexican cuisine with a modern touch."

Appropriation is considered one of America's hallmarks. And Simon says as much. "We are the greatest mutts that history ever put together," he tells the circle. "We drag everything through the collective and it comes out different. We wouldn't have anything without it." He's not wrong, though the emphasis on our melting pot heritage tends to overlook the relative diversity to be found in nations that are not us. And in the context of wealth and power—who has it and who doesn't—America's allegedly unique ability to take in hybridity and generate more of it looks more like the survivalist motivations of capitalism than amity or cosmopolitanism. Appropriation doesn't just make good food, it makes good business sense. If black Americans inspire the demand for hot chicken, than why not buy the more expensive real estate in the busier part of town to attract white tourists, even if you might drive the people with less wealth out of business? Why not take the idea to Shake Shack corporate? If the health of the

economy hinges as much on competition as our legislation suggests, op-
portunistic appropriation is basically a civic duty. While one gray-haired
Texas president drawled about "weapons of mass destruction," the people
soothed themselves with a gray-haired Southern lady and turned her into
a millionaire.

The gears of market and profits make the question of respect so impossibly knotted, even for someone like Bishop or Brock or the non-Chinese
owners of Kings County Imperial or the non-Korean kimchi buffs. White
America is incredibly irresponsible with food. At McSweeney's, the novel-
ist Rajeev Balasubramanyam offers a numbered to do list for appropriation
"nonbelievers":

1. Your new friends Bob and Rita come to lunch and you serve them
   idlis, like your grandmother used to make.
2. They love your South Indian cooking and ask for the recipe.
3. You never hear from Rita and Bob again.
4. You read in the Style section of the *Guardian* about Rita and Bob's
   new Idli bar in Covent Garden . . . *called* Idli.
5. You visit Idli. The food tastes nothing like your grandmother's.
6. Your grandmother dies.
7. Rita and Bob's children inherit the Idli chain, and open several
   franchises in America.
8. Your children find work as short order chefs . . . at Idli.
9. Your children visit you in a nursing home and cook you idlis,
   which taste nothing like the ones you remember from your youth.
10. You compliment their cooking and ask for the recipe.
11. You die.[15]

The dead really get to me. How many dead? How many culinary ge-
niuses died, poor and destitute, without healthcare, trying to live in a
country that only bestows greatness on those a priori deemed great at
birth? How many will die unknown while their recipes live on in the
flavor profiles of some milk-breathed Francophile?

Yet, you are never so far from authenticity as when you think you've
found the one representative for a culture that lives in people, plural.

Culinary historian Michael W. Twitty knows this well. Early in his James Beard Award–winning book *The Cooking Gene: A Journey Through African-American Culinary History in the Old South*, he chides his—mostly white—peers in the field who take to Southern food history as a means of intellectual superiority over contemporary Southerners whose vegetable taxonomy is mostly guided by supermarket stock. "That Lost-Ark-meets-Noah's-ark mentality is intellectually thrilling and highly motivational," Twitty writes, "but it pales in comparison to the task of providing economic opportunity, cultural and spiritual reconnection, improved health and quality of life, and creative and cultural capital to the people who not only used to grow that food for themselves and others, but have historically been suppressed from benefiting from their ancestral legacy."[16]

Twitty knows the many, many scientific and vernacular names for the crops, spices, measurements, dishes, utensils, and techniques of the antebellum cuisine that was an amalgamation of African, Native, and European influences. Twitty was born in Washington, DC, to "an atypical but typical black American family" whose relatives stretched back and forth across the Mason-Dixon Line and out West, also touching various corners around the world. Though he grew up with mustard greens in the sink and yeast rolls in the oven with culinary terms from the *Better Homes and Gardens Encyclopedia of Cooking* on his tongue, Twitty's knowledge comes from the deliberate practice of an adult—the decision to live history through intention. He doesn't give himself the benefit of cooking without ghosts. "I bring all of this into the historical kitchen with me: politics and race, sexuality and spirituality, memory, brokenness, repair, reclamation and reconciliation, and anger." He adds, "It is not enough to know the past of the people you interpret. You must know your own past."

This is the challenge white chefs must enter the ring with if they are ever to deviate from the antiquated methods of their kin, assuming they want to. When people of color challenge white people to dig, they assume *into us* is the silent preposition there. Yes, know our names, know our mama's names and our auntie's names and names of what our enslaved and interned ancestors made. Know the names of the tiny shacks and counter-only joints cooking up god-only-knows what on the low. Know who gets erased, but know your part in it. See yourself in the lineage that fought and killed and gerrymandered its way to being the only name in town. See and understand that, and only upon seeing, really seeing, decide if this lane needs you. Sometimes being the best you can be means stepping aside—let the doing be done.

CHAPTER 8

The Entrepreneur

A Bit Free

The flames soon completed their work, and this handsome struc-
ture, the fruit of old Adam Miller's industry, the monument of
his son's philanthropy, a promise of good things for the future
of the city, lay smouldering in ruins, a melancholy witness to
the fact that our boasted civilization is but a thin veneer, which
cracks and scales off at the first impact of primal passions.

Where a black dollar can be made and saved, white violence follows. "Race riot" is a misnomer. When white people marched on Hard Scrabble in 1824, on Cincinnati in 1826, on Cincinnati in 1829, on Snow Town in 1831, on Cincinnati in 1841, Philly in 1842, on Detroit in 1863, on New Orleans in 1866, on New Orleans in 1879, on Phoenix in 1898, on Wilmington in 1898, on Atlanta in 1906, on Charleston in 1919, on Memphis in 1919, on Macon in 1919, on Bisbee in 1919, on Scranton in 1919, on Philly in 1919, on Longview in 1919, on Baltimore in 1919, on DC in 1919, on Norfolk in 1919, on New Orleans in 1919, on Darby in 1919, on Chicago in 1919, on Bloomington in 1919, on Syracuse in 1919, on Hattiesburg in 1919, on New York in 1919, on Knoxville in 1919, on Omaha in 1919, on Elaine in 1919, on Ocoee in 1920, on Tulsa in 1921, on Perry in 1922, on Detroit in 1943, on Memphis in 1966, on Charlottesville in 2017, it was no more a "race riot" than when twenty-one-year-old Dylann Roof opened fire on the group of twelve gathered in prayer June 17, 2015.

"Race riot" is a distraction. Like a softball thrown into the eye of a hurricane, we've made the phrase matter-of-fact while the maelstrom of history moans all around. The word "race" here, as in so many beloved turns of phrase, omits the matter of who and whom—who attacks whom, who lynches whom, who massacres whom, who bombs whom, who will not rest until breath cannot be sustained by whom in this country. "Riot" is no better, making premeditated murders more resemble crimes of passion, a category of abuses America is inclined to forgive.* There was no reason to call these events other than what they are unless to suspend tragedy and foster disbelief. For, says poet Steve Light, "a term was already in existence which could have been used for the aforementioned attacks and massacres: pogrom."[1] The *Oxford English Dictionary* defines "pogrom," from Russian and Yiddish, as "an organized, officially tolerated, attack on any community or group," originally applied to Russia's organized massacres of Jewish people in the nineteenth century.

America's frequent pogroms were not, just as its many lynchings were not, motivated by the need to defend white women's mythical purity. It has been well over a century since journalist Ida B. Wells dispelled the misbegotten idea that white people had been killing black people all that time solely to preserve their women from some perceived lecherous intent of black men, risking limb and life to do so. White women's chastity was at best an alibi for the roiling white resentment especially inflamed by the mere *prospect* of black progress, no matter how meager. The Emancipation Proclamation was an affront, and Southern Reconstruction a debasement worse than the centuries of enslavement that had preceded it. After the party of Lincoln rolled over and showed its belly in 1877, the white South vowed to make the black South pay. The white South—and North and West and East—still vows it.

Not a "riot" but a "coup d'état," says the author Charles W. Chesnutt in his keen Southern novel, *The Marrow of Tradition*, which Du Bois called "one of the best sociological studies of the Wilmington Riot which I have

---

*Hence the country's abysmal empathy with and protection of domestic abuse victims. America only barely cares about women killed by men, not those hurt by men. And only the women who are white.

seen."[2] Published in 1901, the novel builds out from events that took place in Wilmington, North Carolina, surrounding the November 1898 election. Various groups unofficially associated with the Democratic Party—including Wilmington's "White Government Union," whose constitution expressed its goal to "re-establish in North Carolina the SUPREMACY of the WHITE RACE"—had for months ramped up an intimidation campaign with lethal purpose. There were conventions. One South Carolina senator, Ben Tillman, asked a North Carolina rally why they didn't "kill that nigger editor" already, referring to Alex L. Manly, the editor of the Wilmington *Daily Record*.* Manly had responded in print to a speech given by Mrs. Rebecca Latimer Felton, who supported lynching "a thousand times a week if necessary" as a means of protection.† In the August *Daily Record* editorial, Manly gestured to the hypocrisy of white men, whose claimed protective instincts didn't stop them from abusing and raping their own women themselves. He also, more cheekily, suggested that white men could better blame their predicament on white women's desires and consensual "clandestine meetings with colored men." By early November, mobs of over one-thousand strong regularly patrolled Wilmington's black blocks, shooting at churches, homes, and schools.

In Chesnutt's novelization, the days leading up to what would be called a race riot saw black residents "oiling up the old army muskets" or spiriting themselves away, "disappeared from the town between two suns."[3] Those who remained, in truth as in fiction, faced a mob of two thousand angry whites. The precise number of black dead remains forever unknown. There were no white casualties. In 2006 a state-appointed panel called the 1898 Wilmington Race Riot Commission determined that the violence was not a riot but part of "a documented conspiracy" that "took place within the context of an ongoing statewide political campaign based on white supremacy."[4] In 2007 the North Carolina Democratic Party State Executive Committee passed a resolution renouncing "the bloody massacre." And yet still it is called, like so many of its kind, a riot.

---

* Clemson University's Tillman Hall was named in 1946 for this same Ben Tillman.

† She would, fittingly, go on to be the first woman to serve in the US Senate, elected in 1922 (though she only served one day).

Two decades after Wilmington, bombs rained down upon Tulsa. The Great War was over, but white America's fight for total economic domination is never ending. Early-twentieth-century Greenwood, Oklahoma, was thriving. The black neighborhood north of the tracks put freedom, segregation, and the oil boom to good use, making itself more like a town or small city. There were churches and parks and pharmacies and theaters and gambling halls, lawyers and dentists and sex workers and hoteliers, a movie theater, a library, a high school with instruction in not just grammar and arithmetic but also chemistry and physics. There were fine homes along with more modest accommodations. As in white towns, many of which could not rival Greenwood's development, not everyone in Greenwood was living high off the hog, but making it was possible. Entrepreneurship was possible in a territory attached to the nation with vivid memories of slavery. Historically, Greenwood offers a romantic portrait of what black autonomy did and could look like in Jim Crow America. The nickname it acquired, Negro Wall Street (now black Wall Street), bolsters the vision, like black America's own Gatsby affair located 1300 miles southwest of Harlem.* The 2018 Marvel film release *Black Panther* has since inspired comparisons to the technologically advanced cloistered nation of Wakanda.

And the idea that black people would live, work, build, eat, learn, stroll, and play undisturbed long enough in a place to put a name on it sounds somewhat fantastical. As often as black people are compelled to do the impossible vis-à-vis bootstrapping, achieved impossibility is never allowed to *just be*. Black enterprise does not go unpunished if unaffiliated with white profits. Whiteness will gleefully disturb black neighborhoods, black accolades, black centers, black classrooms, black archives, and black methods. If not allowed to join in—that is, if prevented from profiting from the goings-on—well, the whole thing might as well go up in flames.†

---

*In its day, white people called it "Niggertown," because *of course*.

†A survey cosponsored by NPR in 2017 found that over half of white Americans believe discrimination against white people exists. (Don Gonyea, "Majority of White Americans Say They Believe Whites Face Discrimination," NPR, October 24, 2017.)

The nation was already erupting and Tulsa's white population had only been waiting for their turn. The excuse for trouble started when a black teenage shoe shiner named Dick Rowland shared an elevator with a white teenage elevator attendant named Sarah Page. He said he touched her arm; she said he raped her. Rumors escalated, accusations bandied about. Rowland was arrested and held at the courthouse, trial pending, which in the era of Jim Crow actually meant an expedited sentencing of another kind, sponsored by judge, jury, and Maker. Per tradition, hundreds of armed white people gathered at the courthouse, ready for the lynching. A much smaller number of black residents joined them, concerned for Rowland's fate. A white man ordered a black Great War veteran to turn over his weapon—the veteran did not. A gunshot sounded. Then another and then another. And then it was time for thousands to put their dreams into motion and burn and bomb Greenwood to the ground.

It, too, is called a riot, but there was no disorder here. "Buildings were set on fire systematically, with teams of white rioters gathering flammable materials in the center of a room, dousing them with kerosene, and igniting them," writes *The Ringer*'s Victor Luckerson. "Planes circled overhead—according to police, they were for reconnaissance, but survivors said they dropped bombs filled with turpentine or coal oil."[5] There was also a "roving machine gun that white attackers mounted on a truck." An estimated 100 to 300 people died, with almost a thousand more injured. Though disregard and hatred for black life was evinced by war-grade weapons and fury, the number of dead and permanently injured seems like lucky happenstance. The white mob left 9,000 black Tulsans homeless, but alive. But Greenwood as anyone had known it was gone. Over 1,200 houses were gone, hundreds more looted. Businesses were gone. Page took back her accusation against Rowland and the charges were dropped.

Greenwood rebuilt in spite of its trauma—what else could it do? Some residents fled, to other towns also just a hair's breadth away from white madness and destruction. Rebuilding is difficult under any circumstances and the roadblocks Greenwood encountered communicated how furiously white people wished the neighborhood had never existed in the first place. One ordinance passed by the city of Tulsa, reports Luckerson, required that buildings in Greenwood be two stories tall and fireproof, "a naked attempt to price black residents out of their own community." The contemporary equivalent of $25 million in damages went without restitution. Still, Greenwood rebuilt, roaring through the jazz and blues-filled '20s with the best of them. But no black enterprise can last too long, even one that rose from the ashes. Today, an interstate sits smack down the middle of the neighborhood like the neighborhood doesn't exist. Gentrification encroaches; black people retreat to the margins. That's a more usual tale.

Though Greenwood got its nickname from the New York embodiment of the American financial sector, the community itself exemplified the ways black people lived and still live in the literal and figurative between spaces of Western economy. Largely shut out from making the entirety of a living in professions deemed legal and appropriate, black people have often had to work at the margins of capital to earn enough to live on. These workers include all the people shouted out on Kanye's "Jesus Walks," but also much more mundane, unsensational ventures. The college student doing heads for $20 a pop in her dorm room, food joints ran out the back of someone's house, impromptu swap meets, loosies sold on the train, airbrushed T-shirts designed and made by artisans (who saw none of the profits when Balenciaga decided to sell their aesthetic on an $895 hoodie in 2018). But where a black dollar can be made, white violence follows.

Summer in America means losing your mind. Leading into the summer of 2018, a deeply American meme endeavored to lighten the mood. On April 12, 2018, Philadelphia residents Rashon Nelson and Donte Robinson did something quite ordinary. They walked into their local Starbucks for a business meeting, sat down, and waited for a third acquaintance to arrive. During their wait, a Starbucks employee—name protected by the company—also did something quite ordinary. The employee, a manager, called the police. The police (of course) showed up and "said the guys were 'trespassing,'" recounts a writer named Melissa DePino, who was seated close to what would soon become *a scene*. DePino preemptively corroborated her own witness statement with cell footage of events as they rolled out, footage that (of course) went viral.

The video is disturbing in its calm. The most flushed and indignant occupants of the shot are not the men summarily cuffed within the efficient interior, nor the cops doing the cuffing, but a random white male patron—or assumed patron (it's assumed he's paid for the right to be there while knowing he would still be allowed to be there if he hadn't). "The composition accelerates empathy: the third-party outrage, expressed by the white male citizen, who is assumed to be more sober-headed than the always aggrieved black one, legitimizes our own in a way that the men's first-person testimony would not have," writes Doreen St. Félix. My aversion to videos like this sours my throat. Knowledge of the outcome, that everybody leaves the scene breathing if not well, leaves the moral quandary mostly unchanged. I watch with worry, worry of the risk that some glitch will peel back the statistical plausibility behind the counterfactual playing out before my eyes. Says St. Félix, "The video crystallized the way in which unnecessary 911 calls precipitate the kinds of police interaction that can end catastrophically for black and brown people." That possible catastrophe unsettles the relative serenity captured in bytes. When it comes to encounters with the police, catastrophe is ordinary, a very regular thing.

In the language of meme culture, this very regular thing was transformed so suddenly into an exemplary thing. The recorded moment of two black men removed from a Starbucks located in the City of Brotherly Love became the springboard, as it were, to a grand conversation on the relationship between *white people* and the police. The discussion was helped along with added footage. As if given permission for having an audience, video after video surfaced across the summer months, all on theme and named according to alliterative affiliation. There was "BBQ Becky," the nickname given to Dr. Jennifer Schulte who called the Oakland police on a group of black people grilling in the park. "Pool Patrol Paula," née Stephanie Sebby-Strempel, assaulted a black teen at a community pool in Summerville, South Carolina, before threatening to call the police on him and his friends. "Coupon Carl" of Chicago stammers his profile of Camilla Hudson, who identifies herself on tape and says she "will be waiting" for the cops who've been called on her over an allegedly faulty coupon. Unlike DePino's video, which keeps its eye on the cops, these meme-able enactments make their callers famous. The videos canonize white people as the surrogate cops they are. Uniformed police, if they appear, are secondary or even tertiary to the drama at hand.

For all the lethal potential they contained, there was joy to be found in these videos. They were like anything that might've appeared on *America's Funniest Home Videos*—no matter how gnarly the wipeout, you assumed the person was OK, so the laughter was OK. The humor and its darkness said as much about state violence as those *other* videos, the ones without laughter attached. There was joy to be found because the outcome was known and seemed bent toward some sort of meager justice. If black people are routinely harassed, injured, and killed by white people with the police on speed dial, getting fired is the least these trigger happy fools can do.

Allegedly *not* "fired," Alison Ettel "resigned" from TreatWell Health after she was recorded calling the police on a small black child selling water to passersby on an eighty-degree Saturday in June. Pale, red-nosed, and sweating, Ettel, or "Permit Patty," paces back and forth, hand on hip, phone to her ear like a lifeline. Seeing the telltale signs of a cell camera filming her, she ducks out of view, but the camera finds her anyway. In interviews with the *San Francisco Chronicle* and *Huffington Post*, Ettel claimed she was only fooling, that the call was, after all, fake—supposing her behavior would be somehow appropriate for only *threatening* an eight-year-old black girl. Ettel was lying, of course, as local San Francisco station KRON revealed soon enough. "Hi," Ettel says, greeting the 911 dispatcher like a chipper salesperson, "I'm having someone that, um, does not have a vendor permit that's selling water across from the ballpark." A long pause follows and the call takes on a comedy of its own. The deep voice on the other side of the line responds: "Uhhhhhh."

Among the cast of characters accumulated during those sweltering months, Ettel was specially egregious for certain off-camera proclivities, namely her profession. Until she decided to sic the cops on a child, Ettel was the CEO of TreatWell, which she founded and launched in 2015. TreatWell makes cannabis tinctures for humans and animals. The company's pet tinctures, per its website, "blend . . . extracts with MCT oil (fractionated coconut oil) and wild salmon oil for ease of digestion, added health benefits and a taste most dogs and cats love." Despite the controversial nature of medicinal marijuana for pets—both the ASPCA and the

American Veterinary Medical Association are hesitant if not outright skeptical—Ettel promoted the animal-focused side of TreatWell efficaciously. Featured in an article called "Pot for Your Pup?" Ettel told the *San Francisco Chronicle* that "many of her patients are informally recommended to her from Bay Area veterinarians (who can't officially administer marijuana treatments under federal law)."[6] On the legal gray area, "It's kind of like 'don't ask, don't tell,'" she said in 2015. "We haven't gotten any pushback yet." By next year, *Edibles* magazine—*yes*—named her "one of the leading experts" on cannabis for pets.[7] The contortion required is too much. In a country that arrests black people for marijuana possession at four times the rate of white people who enjoy weed so much they give their doggos a chance to get high, Ettel, a proud pusher, staged a criminal encounter with a black child giving water to baseball fans to raise money for a trip to Disney World. It's hysterical.

Months later, TreatWell quietly rebranded under the name Rosette Wellness. "We have restructured with new management, fresh new look, while keeping the same exact quality & product lines you can trust," the company tweeted.

The history of weed in America is, as even the most sanitized accounts will tell, *complicated.* Which, as the most sanitized accounts won't tell, is a euphemism for America's racism, which girded the antidrug legislation that translated a mostly benign recreational habit into a federal offense. The history of weed in America doesn't really begin until the early twentieth century. The psychotropic species of cannabis have been known to peoples around the world for several millennia, but what is relevant to the way we talk about weed in America today derives from the moment when weed became brown and thus dangerous and thus necessarily purged from this nation.

The year is 1930. Harry J. Anslinger, thirty-eight, is appointed the first commissioner of the Federal Bureau of Narcotics by President Herbert Hoover. Arriving at the tail of Prohibition, Anslinger would soon nurse nationwide hysteria over another substance, with just the right scapegoats to make it stick. The genuine origins of the drug now on US soil made for a convincing starting point. Even the colloquial "marihuana," borrowed from Spanish, intensified the sense that the drug, like the places and people whence it came, was exotic, but malignant. Anslinger compiled a docket of evidence stacked against the drug now known as the Gore File—books and audiotapes and clipping after clipping documenting the misbegotten and often murderous exploits of people allegedly under the influence of weed.

Such an archive, now more the tenor of urban mythology, likely provided the source material for Anslinger's article "Marijuana, Assassin of Youth," published by the *American Magazine* in 1937. He begins with a bang:

> The sprawled body of a young girl lay crushed on the sidewalk the other day after a plunge from the fifth story of a Chicago apartment house. Everyone called it a suicide, but actually it was murder. The killer was a narcotic known to America as marijuana, and to history as hashish. It is a narcotic used in the form of cigarettes, comparatively new to the United States and as dangerous as a coiled rattlesnake.[8]

The story behind the lede offers only vague details to color the narrative. "Her story is typical," Anslinger writes. The girl and her friends came together to try a new type of cigarette and each took a few drags. "The results were weird," though probably familiar to anyone who's ever been high, and "every remark, no matter how silly, seemed excruciatingly funny. Others of mediocre musical ability became almost expert. . . . Still others found themselves discussing weighty problems of youth with remarkable clarity." Our *girl*—no name given—"danced without fatigue, and the night of unexplainable exhilaration seemed to stretch out as though it were a year long." But blissful as this may seem, dear reader, we already know the ending to this tale. "Finally," the young girl partakes on a night when her head is elsewhere, concerned about her flagging studies. "With every puff of the smoke the feeling of despondency lessened" and "in the midst of laughter and dancing she thought of her school problems. Instantly they were solved. Without hesitancy, she walked to the window and leaped to her death."

Anslinger doesn't identify the race of the mystery victim, nor does he need to for readers to know the young girl is white. Anslinger never explicitly mentions race at all, relying instead on suggestion to get the job done. All he needs is contrast, the sanctified American family (white) versus the seedy, unregulated underbelly (dark). In the article's staging, the "hot tamale vendor" or "street peddler" are the coiled desert snakes ready to pounce on America's promising youth; they come from "the Southwest" and lurk not only on the streets of these American states but "in a dance hall or over a lunch counter"; they might even be the "school janitor." Anslinger claims marijuana dates back to the ancient Greeks, since then appropriated by tribal groups who've capitalized on the drug's alleged induced violence, from the ancient Egyptians to the Persians to Arabic-language speakers to the indigenous people of the Malay Peninsula. From there, "Marijuana was introduced into the United States from Mexico, and swept across America with incredible speed," he writes. Without a stop to the menace, he implies, the United States will fall to the depths of barbarity akin to these ethnic states. Local and state-level laws weren't enough, Anslinger argued; only "the powerful right arm" of "the United States government," a "national law against the growing, sale, or possession of marijuana," could contend with the problem at hand. Fear-mongering worked. Not one month later the Marihuana Tax Act of 1937 was enacted by Congress. Though the act in name only imposed taxes on the sale and distribution of marijuana, in practice it made possession criminal.

Of special concern to Anslinger was the way music of a certain kind made itself receptive to weed and weed smokers. "Among those who first introduced it there were musicians," he claimed, "who had brought the habit northward with the surge of 'hot' music demanding players of exceptional ability, especially in improvisation." In the 1937 article he writes rather artfully about the effect of weed on, as he says, "the musical sensibilities":

> The musician who uses "reefers" finds that the musical beat seemingly comes to him quite slowly, thus allowing him to interpolate any number of improvised notes with comparative ease. While under the influence of marijuana, he does not realize that he is tapping the keys, with a furious speed impossible for one in a normal state of mind; marijuana has stretched out the time of the music until a dozen notes may be crowded into the space normally occupied by one.

Anslinger does not here mention the jazzman by name, but the chill then frenetic improvisational style full of notes that conform to no earthly measure can only be jazz and its infinite forms, the black sound sweeping the nation and ensnaring white youth much as he thought marijuana was. In other forums he was more candid, making reference to Harlem nightclubs and performers such as Cab Calloway in his memos; he opened files dedicated to keeping tabs on prominent black musicians. In 1949 testimony before the House Appropriations Committee, Anslinger repeated his rhetoric from the decade before, speaking of increases in traffic "particularly among young people."[9] Additionally, he said, "we have been running into a lot of traffic among these jazz musicians, and I am not speaking about the good musicians, but the jazz type."[10] In 1956, in the wake of *Brown v. Board of Education* and while civil rights legislation was being considered, Anslinger testified to a House subcommittee the dubious statistic that "60 percent of drug addicts in the United States are Negroes."[11]

The bureau under Anslinger followed his prejudices. Lacking immediate access to the black enclaves that, to him, uniquely housed the cause of all the country's problems (in person and plant form), Anslinger made use of informants who would blend in and take cash for their trouble. "He bought his way into a culture that, by its very nature, he had despised from the start," writes Larry Sloman in *Reefer Madness: The History of Marijuana in America*, "and tried to silence it by arresting its members for their usage of an herb."[12] One of the bureau's victims was Lady Day herself, Billie Holiday, targeted by Anslinger from her first onstage performances of "Strange Fruit" in the late '30s to her deathbed at New York's Metropolitan Hospital in 1959.[13] Anslinger presided over the bureau for thirty-two years under Hoover, then FDR, then Harry Truman, then Dwight Eisenhower, then JFK, finally departing at the age of seventy. He left behind relics of the lives his representatives hounded and, indeed, the strengthened arm of a government already predisposed to destroy black lives.

This is the mantle that would be taken up by LBJ, Richard Nixon, Reagan, and the Clintons. In his 1995 memoir, *Dreams from My Father*, Barack Obama disclosed his experience with smoking weed, a biographical tidbit resurrected a decade later in the run-up to the 2008 presidential election. As president, he curved away from the militant language of his predecessors, instead comparing weed to nicotine and alcohol, legal substances with the potential for abuse. Obama granted clemency to 1,927 people by the end of his final term, most of whom had been imprisoned for nonviolent drug crimes.[14] And yet, despite his administration's refusing the rhetorical inheritance of his predecessors at the federal level, the war on drugs continued unabated. A report conducted by the American Civil Liberties Union and Human Rights Watch found that in 2015 "nearly half of all drug possession arrests (over 574,000) were for marijuana possession."[15] Though black people and white people light up at about the same rate, and white people are more likely to partake of illicit substances overall, black people are arrested for drug possession at much, much higher rates than whites.* In Alaska, where recreational weed has been legal since 2014, of the seventeen—*seventeen*—total marijuana arrests in 2016, black people made up 29 percent while making up less than 4 percent of the state's population.[16] In both Manhattan, where recreational use of marijuana is illegal, and Washington, DC, where it is legal, black people are eleven times as likely as white people to be arrested for possession of weed.[17]

In the words of Anslinger, "That's marijuana!"[18]

Nearly ninety years after Anslinger took up his post, the weed business is booming. So much so that the Green Rush, the surge of commercial opportunities opening up in the sale of weed, will soon be old news. Weed remains illegal under federal law, classified, along with heroine and LSD, as a schedule 1 drug: "defined as drugs with no currently accepted medical use and a high potential for abuse."[19] Nearly two-thirds of states, however, have progressively legalized various types of usage and sale of the drug, pushing its legality into a gray area for much of the nation. As laws have shifted so has public opinion, dissolving stereotypes and taboos and thus expanding the market. The legal industry was valued at over $10 billion in the US in 2018, estimated to grow by at least $30 billion over the next decade. The jazzman turned pusher—"harsh, predatory,

---

*For the thirty-nine states that provide sufficient arrest data to the FBI, the report determined that black adults are more than four times as likely to be arrested for marijuana possession than white adults. In Iowa and Vermont, where black people make up less than 5 percent of the population, black adults were more than six times as likely to be arrested for possession as whites.

cruel"—has become The Guy, "a white hipster Jesus in a bike helmet," writes Niella Orr.[20] The Guy is not only the protagonist of the web show turned HBO series *High Maintenance* following the fictional adventures of an anonymous weed dealer in Brooklyn, he is an archetype, says Orr, "redrawing the public face of pot dealing in America."[21] The Guy as well as his clientele—white and secure, if not well-off—is joined by beloved stoners Abby and Ilana of *Broad City*, together the composite for a newly visible class of lady weed enthusiasts.

The truth is even more fanciful than pop culture. Dispensaries now resemble boutique grocery stores, one-stop shops for all things cannabis. Today, the weed business is so much more than kush: portable vape pens and tinctures, "cannabis-infused" salted caramel almonds and sour apple gummy bears. There are weed critics and connoisseurs, weed magazines, weed yoga classes taught by off-duty Equinox instructors, multiday weed conferences, weed weddings and bud bars, 22-karat-gold-dipped one-hitters for $75 and sterling silver grinders for $1,475. Cannabidiol (CBD), a nonpsychoactive cannabinoid found in cannabis, has taken off in a boom of its own, spreading to beauty aisles, pharmacies, juice bars, and pet stores. CBD providers also operate in a gray region, legally and bodily. While product pushers are effusive over the effects of CBD— promised to reduce anxiety, smooth wrinkles, relieve soreness and pain, mitigate chronic health conditions, and more—skeptics wonder whether companies provide high enough doses to reap the compound's benefits, or whether CBD does anything at all. "The problem is," writes the *Atlantic*'s Amanda Mull, "it's not easy to know what you're actually ingesting, or if it'll actually change how you feel."[22]

As weed becomes so mainstream as to make puffing passé, it's become easy to overlook the legality of the matter.* Weed is only contingently legal, even in states with fairly liberal positions on possession, and yet the

---

*While widespread knowledge of Obama's weed-smoking days seemed to improve his reputation, becoming the subject of a sketch on *Key & Peele* in 2012 ("Obama—The College Years"), presidential candidate Kamala Harris's admission on the radio show *The Breakfast Club* several years later ("Kamala Harris Interview and More," February 11, 2019) felt forced to many who thought it was an already belated attempt at garnering approval from young black voters.

asides journalists and trend forecasters once dedicated to the contradiction of legal weed in America shrink and shrink, if included at all. It becomes less morally relevant to remind readers, consumers, and voters of all the people imprisoned, those who have been convicted and those who simply cannot make bail, for possession of a product now bought and sold at Barneys.* As the makeup of the market attests, only certain kinds of people are able to take advantage of the gray, the same kinds of people for whom the law has always been more suggestion than fact. Obama's relative lenience—which still saw millions arrested—was a dream state quickly dissolved in 2017 when the Trump administration took the helm. In May 2017, Attorney General Jeff Sessions overrode former attorney general Eric Holder's 2013 memo, which advised prosecutors against pressing charges for nonviolent, isolated drug offenses.[23] In the 2017 memo, Sessions mandates prosecutors "charge and pursue the most serious, readily provable offense," warning that "any decision to vary from the policy must be approved by a United States Attorney or Assistant Attorney General."[24] Marijuana is increasingly decriminalized across the country, yet the number of marijuana arrests is rising. On February 15, 2019, after Congress refused to allocate $5 billion to pay for a wall spanning the length of the 1,954 mile-long border between Mexico and the United States, the president declared a national emergency to seize funds. "One of the things I said I have to do and I want to do is border security," the president said, "because we have tremendous amounts of drugs flowing into our country, much of it coming from the southern border."[25]

Even in communities where the drone of presidential xenophobia and racism feels far away, the weed business remains out of reach for black and brown experts who've risked the most to learn their craft. Perhaps as an overcorrection due to the tenuous nature of the law, states that have legalized weed for medical or recreational use prohibit people with drug offenses on their record from being involved in a cannabis business in any

---

*In February 2019 the luxury department chain announced it would open an upscale head shop called High End at its Beverly Hills location, with other California stores to follow, in partnership with Beboe, the weed supplier known as the "Hermès of marijuana." High-end customers can place in-store orders for delivery.

way. (In my state, Illinois, people with drug felonies are not even allowed to be medical marijuana *patients*.) A survey published by *Marijuana Business Daily* in 2017 found that just 10 percent of respondents who founded or possessed an ownership stake in a cannabis business identified as Latino or African American.[26] "Yes, investors and state governments are eager to hire and license people with expertise in how to cultivate, cure, trim, and process cannabis. But it can't be someone who got caught. Which for the most part means it can't be someone who is black," surmised reporter Amanda Chicago Lewis in a *BuzzFeed* investigation of racial disparities in the Green Rush.[27] The black and brown people running weed businesses most endangered and devastated by busts, who, like their forebears, created opportunities in the interstices of American propriety in order to get by, are systematically prevented from thriving now that the business is out in the open. Weed, originally criminalized for being too Mexican and too black, now sheds its racial residue without reparations. (Amnesia strikes again.)

Owing to initiatives by local activists, some cities and states have instituted programs designed to improve parity. In California, Oakland's Equity Permit Program promises at least half of its licenses to Oakland residents who've either incurred a weed conviction in the city since 1996 or lived in neighborhoods "with disproportionately higher number of cannabis-related arrests."[28] Similar, if softer, programs have appeared in Massachusetts, Ohio, and Pennsylvania. Recreational use is still illegal in Maryland, but State's Attorney Marilyn Mosby announced in early 2019 that marijuana possession would no longer be prosecuted in Baltimore. "Communities are still sentenced under these unjust policies, still paying a price for behavior that is already legal for millions of Americans," she said.[29] And as New York moves toward legalization, New York politicians such as Congresswoman Alexandria Ocasio-Cortez and Democratic gubernatorial primary candidate Cynthia Nixon have taken the position that the topic of race is inextricable from the topic of legal weed. During her 2018 gubernatorial debate with Governor Andrew Cuomo, Nixon called legalization "a racial justice issue," one that ought to "prioritize the communities that have been most harmed by the War on Drugs." Equity goes beyond awarding licenses, Nixon noted, and includes financial support. She added, "We need to parole people who are in jail for marijuana arrests and we need to expunge their records and use some of this tax revenue [from legal marijuana] for them to reenter [the business]."

Financially, the barriers to entry into weed commerce look a lot like the barriers that have kept black people from authorized commercial activity since ever. Weed's first movers are not only white but well funded. "Getting funded is a bitch," Wanda James told *Vice*'s Benjamin Goggin.[30] James, Colorado's first black dispensary owner, recalls minimum start-up costs upwards of $250,000 when she got her start in 2009. Speaking with Goggin nearly a decade later, those costs had since run up into millions at a minimum, and business owners cannot count on bank loans for a federally illegal pursuit. Even with diversity initiatives at the licensing level, "The only way for black and brown small business people to enter is if you can partner with a large funded white business," Amber Senter, cofounder of Supernova Women, which uplifts women of color in the weed business, told Goggin.[31] Additionally, black people and other people of color already in on the legal side of the industry are uniquely burdened with issues of reparations and inequality compared to their white peers. Kadeesha, cofounder of the Metropolitan Collective, told *Refinery29* of several "unprofessional" encounters at conferences, instigated by white men who prefer to hit on her than network or discuss issues of race and gender.[32] Rina Cakrani, a Whitman College student, wrote in 2018, "Everyone should feel uncomfortable with how white America is setting up generational wealth off of weed when so many Black and Latino men have been incarcerated and lost their livelihood over the same thing"—yet remorse among proprietors runs low.[33] As David Bruno, leader of a failed bid to legalize weed in Ohio in 2015, told Chicago Lewis, "We're not a nice society, and there's not going to be reparations."[34]

And as white "potrepreneurs" disavow reparations, the mere suggestion of the subject also harms legalization efforts among the general public. In an essay in *The Stranger*, a white reporter, Dominic Holden, revisits his participation in the campaign for Seattle's Initiative 75, a 2003 measure to make weed possession the lowest priority for police enforcement. Holden, who didn't even smoke at the time, advocated for I-75 as a racial-justice matter. Campaign consultants more or less told Holden that this was a bad idea.

> Because we could run that campaign, if we wanted. But that campaign probably wouldn't win. The polling was clear: Those aren't the messages that convince voters to relax the rules for pot. Nobody made us do anything we didn't want to do, but we wanted to win, so we mostly shut up about that race stuff.[35]

Instead, I-75 became about saving time and reducing paperwork, empowering cops to focus on "protecting our communities from serious and violent crime." I-75 passed with the approval of 58 percent of the votes. Legal weed not as reparations but another means for white people to get rich and high.

Weed is not the only place where legal gray areas grease the way for white entrepreneurs to *make it* in a big way. At the 2018 State of the Black Tech Ecosystem conference in Chicago, the author and entrepreneur Felecia Hatcher compared extralegal workarounds like jitney cabs and Malachi Jenkins and Roberto Smith's Trap Kitchen to gig-economy wunderkinder like Uber, Lyft, and Grubhub. Many companies that rely on apps to connect with their customers skirt the issue of licenses and certifications, while black workers caught working around legislation are not so favored. In Tennessee, for example, aggressive cosmetology regulations require hair braiders to be licensed "natural hair stylists" to legally do cornrows, Senegalese twists, or any other popular chemical-free styles.[36] Failure to get a license results in exorbitant fines. The licensing requires expensive instruction at cosmetology school, yet few schools in the state offer such courses. The fines demonstrate no concern for black people and their hair, but rather the felt threat of black labor practices outside the state's reach.

These appropriated ventures have not disrupted the hustle so much as normalized it. What started as creative but necessary means to make a dollar away from Uncle Sam's roving eye have increasingly entered the domain of moguls who act like close-fisted pimps. Tech companies wrest away these means in order to further devalue workers by allowing customers to underpay for services. They leave the working poor—usually black and brown folks hanging on to urban life by a thread—with two choices: join and work for pennies, or be pushed out from the trade, from the neighborhood, from the block that used to be theirs. Some go with the first, some with the second, and most choose a bit of both, adding another notch to their hustle and finding other undetected ways to feel a bit free.

Instagram is not the most intuitive place to sell wares online or purchase someone else's. But when, on May 18, 2015, Nicki Minaj and Beyoncé dropped the video for "Feelin' Myself," it wasn't Poshmark or Facebook or even Etsy people ran to for their choice player's jersey-turned-bodysuit. When the camera panned over Beyoncé Giselle Knowles Carter lying resplendent on a pool floatie with Rose's #1 on her abdomen, the real ones knew exactly where to find unauthorized replicas of Bey and Nick's hood-girl fashions. That place was Instagram. And Instagram merchants, black girls with the prophetic eye for trends, delivered.

Old school and new converge at the Instagram boutique. Like so much online, the origin of the term "Instagram boutique" is hard to pinpoint, though it's been in search engines as early as 2012. By 2015, they were prevalent enough for *The Source*'s Angela Wilson to pen a "Do's and Don'ts of Starting an Instagram Boutique."[37] Instagram boutiques take a variety of forms within the uncompromising template of Facebook's third most popular application. One person sells screen-printed T-shirts with neo-Black-Power-isms; another turns white Chucks into vibrant works of art; another sells wigs, ready to wear or made to order; another does the same, but for queens, creating cascades the color of bubblegum pink, white-blond bouffants, whatever style and color comes to mind; someone else might sell shapewear, someone else a workout plan; all the jewelry and all clothes—party clothes, gym clothes, fan apparel, swim trunks, bikinis, socks, club apparel, designer dupes, original designs, prom dresses, wedding dresses, dresses with cutouts here and here.

There were already dozens of well-known destinations to sell fashions online by the time Instagram launched, and nothing about the app's official interface or tagline—"Capturing and sharing the world's moments"—suggested future entrepreneurs could stake a meaningful claim there. But it makes sense that they would. Brick-and-mortar ownership is almost exclusively limited to the affluent and wealthy, or to those deemed trustworthy enough to secure a loan.[38] Even if banks were lining up to offer small-business loans to black people—they are not—time is not a resource on hand for the many boomers and millennials living paycheck to paycheck. Dot-com businesses, too, require resources in the digital age. Domains are expensive, hosting even more so, and long gone are the days when a little HTML and basic Javascript were all an amateur needed to blend in with the big dogs.* Even as blogging platforms like Blogger and WordPress made it possible to create other sorts of websites for free, the question of promoting one's brand—the most expensive question—remained.

Social media lowered the stakes. As the world went digital, black business found its own lane once again.

Twenty-three-year-old Angie Nwandu had a modest goal: gain ten thousand followers in a year on the Instagram account she started as a writing outlet apart from poetry and screenwriting. While media old and new were panicking, she was sketching out an entertainment destination on par with *TMZ*, *In Touch Weekly*, or *Page Six*. It would not only live on Instagram but take advantage of its shared residence on the platform that had quickly become the place for celebrities to break news on their terms. Nwandu was young, but a practiced writer—she'd finished the script for a film called *Night Comes On*, which had led to an acceptance to the Sundance Screenwriters Lab earlier that year. And better than youth, Nwandu knew the social rhythms of life online. She knew the new vernacular ushered in by social media, where a like or an unfollow speaks volumes and relationships vanish or emerge with all the fanfare of a new profile picture. "Famous people might have regained some control of their public personas through social media, but this has only opened the door to a new form of gossip reporting," wrote the *New York Times Magazine*'s Jenna Wortham in a profile of Nwandu in 2015.[39] The Shade Room

---

*RIP Geocities.

(TSR) was introduced to the world a year prior. The account reached 10,000 followers within two weeks.

Years removed from that auspicious beginning, the idea that the social media activities of celebrities could prove newsworthy sounds like common sense. Reports on the commander in chief's activities—and on those of other government officials—cite his Twitter account more often than anything with an official letterhead. When I scroll through newsfeeds on whatever platform, I am as likely to see friends and acquaintances screenshot an article and upload that screenshot to share their thoughts as see the link to the story itself. New media sites generate listicles full of famous tweets and one racist tweet in the public eye can outshine whole decades' worth of hate speech—enough to kill a primetime network television show. Publishers from low to high brow, national to local, Pulitzer or no, are borrowing techniques from those seedy websites called content aggregators. Content *is* content and shitpics have value. If you gather it, they will come. Natural, if bleak, as that all sounds, not everyone foresaw the change. Nwandu did. In a profile of Nwandu written for *BuzzFeed*, Doree Shafrir mused that Nwandu "might be the first media mogul of the distributed content age."[40] As I write this, over fourteen million accounts follow TSR on Instagram, with millions more spread across other platforms and millions more, I'm sure, by the time you read this sentence.

As a media entity, TSR engenders intimacy with its audience—indeed, as if a close friend has welcomed you onto their chaise to spill some fresh gossip. The posts are simple, even juvenile, the square photos nearly cropped in half by a thick white border bearing the headline in black serif font. Something you might assume was made with MS Paint *before* Microsoft updated its features—or on a smartphone. Following from online fan culture's perpetual standoms, readers are called the "roommates." Nwandu explains, "We call them that because they 'live' in The Shade Room, many of them visit our website/pages every day!" Familiarity is part of the brand, offering a level of transparency unusual even for new media ventures courting millennial and Gen-Z demographics. "Our style of delivering the story is similar to the way a friend or roommate would deliver the story to you. We don't use proper grammar all of the time and we have fun with our writing."

I open Instagram, type S-H-A-D-E, and click on username theshade-room, which is verified with the prized blue checkmark. I embiggen one post and see the screencap of a tweet from Quavo, of Migos:

I Wanna Build A HighSchool
Name It HUNCHO High
"Leaders Are Made."

In the caption TSR asks, "What y'all think his school would be like?" with an emoji at the end, a pair of eyes peeping camera left. I am late—the post has already accumulated over six thousand comments. Some are parodic verses written in Quavo's idiosyncratic flow, complete with ad libs. Others verge on preachy, preemptively on the defense against the jeers they know accompany any post about a celebrity anywhere, but especially on TSR. One user answers the question simply: "Lit lol."

Part of the TSR feeling is the nature of its subjects, who is considered a celebrity when its #Roommates step inside. These are not, for the most part, the impervious Hollywood elite, the Jennifer Lawrences and Ryan Goslings of today's entertainment industry. The figures who frequent so many TSR updates more usually fall into the category of "black famous," a label used disparagingly that is also indicative of a whole world adjacent to the Hollywood celebrity machine. The white community may not remember *Moesha* or *Full Moon*—a banger—or whatever was going on with Brandy and Monica in the '90s, but TSR readers welcome Brandy's contemporary melodramas with open arms. Some, including plenty of black people, may not care about rappers Joe Budden and Lupe Fiasco beefing in Instagram comments, but TSR readers do.

TSR has anointed a new class of stars who reside somewhere inside the triangulation of internet fame, reality television, and fame by association. Ex-partners, side partners, grown children, siblings, parents, in-laws, business partners, washed-up producers—newsworthiness no longer requires celebrity. A woman named Tokyo Toni appears on TSR so regularly that posts involving her no longer explain why she, the mother to Blac Chyna and grandmother to Dream Kardashian, is a topic of conversation. When a woman named Yaya announced she could no longer be counted among

Floyd Mayweather's girlfriends via Instagram Stories' Q&A feature, TSR reposted the story with the caption, "Sis says she's out the players club for good!" When Rick Ross's girlfriend Briana Camille gave birth to the couple's first child, TSR broke the news. And when, almost a year later, the mother of Ross's first child, Tia Kemp, aired dirty laundry regarding Ross's fatherly neglect on Instagram Live, TSR was ready to record and repost. TSR is the pettiest of time capsules

Though it didn't take too long for Nwandu to be recognized by other national news media, including *Forbes* magazine's 30 Under 30 feature, there's an irreverent tone reserved for TSR that is out of step with its meteoric rise. Even podcasters who self-admittedly source the majority of their topics from TSR can't refrain from snarling the name, as if nobody with anything significant going on in their lives would give the Instagram page any mind. TSR is a gossip rag through and through, with unsavory ethics to boot. But its niche format is duplicated all across the web. There's a plainness about it I can't help but respect. In the land where media giants are toppled nearly every day, where the last organizations standing still refuse to diversify their newsroom expertise, Nwandu built a contender with wit and the 'gram. It's not so pretty, but gossip was always just this, wasn't it? Pixelated photos of petty situations people can project onto: nothing more, nothing less.

Black hustlers on Instagram, like black hustlers anywhere, have been seen. Platforms and brands have caught up. It is no longer novel to think digitally and socially together or use the grassroots-like feel of the internet to sell something. In mid-2016, Instagram announced the addition of business profiles. Users could convert their personal profiles into commerce-minded ones and gain access to new tools such as analytics about engagement and growth. Later that year, Instagram began rolling out "shoppable" photo tags for select profiles and told *The Verge* in 2018 that the company was working on a stand-alone shopping app. In 2019, the app added its in-app checkout feature. The big brands—Nike, Zara, H&M, Michael by Michael Kors—seized the opportunity, but many much smaller brands still run their boutiques the old-fashioned way. Instagram's business tools are not available to *just anybody*. Businesses must be legitimated by Facebook's extensive commerce policies, which restrict the type of items sold as well as the advertising content. Would-be merchants must also "grant Facebook a non-exclusive, transferable, sub-licensable, royalty-free, worldwide license to use any data, content, and other information provided . . . including photos, videos, and Product Listing content."*

Black ingenuity lives on. People online find other inventive ways, some truly radical, to feel a bit free. In July 2017 Oakland-based writer, director, and social engineer Dr. Kortney Ryan Ziegler tweeted, "An app that converts your daily change into bail money to free black people." By November, Ziegler and Tiffany Mikell, a software engineer and entrepreneur, launched Appolition, a portmanteau combining "app" and "abolition." The app collects spare change from purchases made and donates the money to the National Bail Out collective, a network of organizations that post bail for people detained without conviction because they cannot afford freedom. Pretrial detention can span weeks, months, and years, effectively jailing people for poverty. Within a justice system that incarcerates black people at disproportionately high rates, bail exacerbates the divide between who is protected from the worst of the state and who is abused by the state. On average seven hundred thousand people every day are "innocent until proven guilty," yet confined to a cell away from their lives, at risk of losing them—to trauma, police maltreatment, physical illness, physical abuse. Both Appolition and National Bail Out seek abolition, an end to mass incarceration, period, while using the resources they can to be reparative in the present system. After nine months, Appolition raised over $200,000 from the spare change in users' digital spare pockets.

As Black Wall Street is memorialized in thought and history and the feature film that will almost certainly come about someday, there is good reason to depart from the capital-tinged vision of what was. Black Wall Street deserves a new name, or maybe its own name, Greenwood, an island like so many black islands, that did what it would.

---

*Scary language and all, the agreement is only an extension of existing Instagram Terms of Use in which you, ordinary user, grant the platform "a non-exclusive, royalty-free, transferable, sub-licensable, worldwide license to host, use, distribute, modify, run, copy, publicly perform or display, translate, and create derivative works of your content (consistent with your privacy and application settings)."

CHAPTER 9

The Activist

The Time for Anger

"Listen," pleaded Mrs. Carteret. "You will not let my baby die! You are my sister;—the child is your own near kin!"

White people are amazing optimists. Greg hasn't spoken with Steve about partisan matters in a decade, but will absolutely throw his hand on a blade to declare Steve "a good guy." Steve could be a Nazi. Steve *probably is* a Nazi. But he's at your election party, so probably, *hopefully*, he is not. Most likely Greg makes too much money, is too male or too white, to care one way or the other.

White optimism is a killer.

On that ecstatic Tuesday millions upon millions lined up and cast their ballot for the candidate who would be the first woman president this country ever saw. Many women, many of them white and denied their shot by the black contingent two cycles ago, took to social media that day, smiling, laughing, crying. Some took daughters to the polls, some took grandmothers, perhaps a little too confident that Granny would hew to liberalism behind the closed curtain. Much as in that other election, the one that taught us to hope, the "I Voted" stickers glimmered that day— incredibly even more laden with political symbolism.

I went to bed early that evening, as I do most evenings. Election parties are not my cup of tea, something I say without ever having been to one, because I can't imagine wanting to be surrounded by a bunch of people in my keenest abjection. Of course, nobody who ever plans an election party ever imagines that outcome. Nor do they consider that the friends and colleagues they interact with daily, whom they've invited into their home, might not be of one mind.

I went to bed that evening and woke up to the sound of the sky falling. Fearful group messages, nauseous tweets, anger, dread, and disappointment. The specifics are hazy. The rest of that year and most of the next my body was racked with near daily panic attacks, unchecked irritability, and a primal need to write something meaningful, sustained, and physical, lest I was not too much longer for this world. My writing suffered. My thinking suffered. Worse, my relationships suffered. I remember frantic calls for anyone with a uterus to get an IUD up there lickity split, like some sort of time capsule to be removed under a much less femicidal regime. I remember the results circulated over and again: She won the popular vote! *Fifty-two percent of white women voted for him. Almost half of white college graduates voted for him. Millennial or boomer, white voters of all ages voted for him.*＊ I remember feeling no small amount of bitterness about these results.

I remember the grasping. Conservatives crowing. Liberals reaching every which way, discombobulated. White men screeching at white women and black Democrats, anybody they blamed for holding their failed male candidate's feet to the fire on trivial matters like racial and reproductive justice. White women chastising the men—all men—so certain misogyny lost them their turn yet again, too distraught to consider how much whiteness had won. Everyone was tossed out of the electoral binary and scattered to the wind.

People who never in a million years thought they'd live to see their personhood interrogated found their faith in the America project bristle for the first time. They were frantic for a language, an action to absolve

---

＊These somewhat apocryphal figures have been subject to adjustment in the years since the election. In 2016, the Pew Research Center, borrowing numbers from CNN.com, reported, "Trump won whites with a college degree 49% to 45%," compared to Clinton (Alec Tyson and Shiva Maniam, "Behind Trump's Victory," Pew Research Center, November 9, 2016). In its own survey conducted in 2016 and published in 2018, Pew found that 38 percent of white college graduates voted for Trump.) (Pew Research Center, *For Most Trump Voters, "Very Warm" Feelings for Him Endured* [August 2018]).

the creeping, climbing suspicion that their optimism had been misplaced. I remember the rallies. I remember the call to action sounded by people who were not yet ready to give up the good ship lollipop: "Love Trumps Hate."*

The momentum was contagious. The people were rallying. The people were angry. Pristine, apolitical Instagram and Facebook pages were sullied with colorful witticisms to convey the radical truth that women are people, too. Plans for a march emerged. The Million Woman March it was to be called. Never mind that the Million Woman March had already taken place in 1997, when hundreds of thousands of women marched on Benjamin Parkway in Philadelphia to assert the then- and still-radical claim that women of African descent across the planet are people, too. Never mind that the original Million Woman March had scheduled a twentieth-anniversary march for that same year. Those who pointed out the overlap were subject to suspicion and outright wrath. Apparently, black women's activism was beside the point. The name was changed after all, to the Women's March on Washington (borrowing from another black-led gathering).

But, the people were marching! Like those black and white photos permitted to sparsely dot schoolchildren's history books. Lots and lots of people in dozens of cities across America came together physically and across cyberspace to protest the onset of a fascist regime absolutely bent on destroying the lives of women who cannot outspend its policies. The unusually warm and sunny January day in Chicago couldn't deter the sorority from their knitted wool pussyhats, a cisterhood of bright-pink kitty ears symbolic of the pink genitalia they marched to protect. Their signs brought social media slogans to life:

"HEY TRUMP, WOMEN ARE PEOPLE, TOO."
"#GRAB AMERICA BACK"
"BUILD A UTERINE WALL"
"THIS PUSSY GRABS BACK"

---

*When chanted over and over in a steady rhythm, the affirmation loses its contours. The verb grows harder to discern: is it "love" or is it "trump"? The assertion, our love will conquer hate, quickly revolves into an appeal to give Trump's hate a chance.

"THE FUTURE IS FEMALE"
"GIRLS JUST WANT TO HAVE FUN-DAMENTAL
    HUMAN RIGHTS"

And as the day wore on and the selfies rolled in, a composite emerged.
The image was not comprehensive, not fair to the full range of those present, but that's a composite. Observers, on the in- and outside, called it as
they saw it. They described the march as very white, very middle class,
very cis, very straight and became enemies of the very feminist ambitions
of the Women's March for their trouble. Critics were expected to wave off
videos and images showing marchers high-fiving cops, taking photos with
cops, of cops in pussyhats. The irony that a march against the state was
applauded *by the state* was not only ignored, but promoted as the crown
feature of the Women's March. Unlike all those *other* demonstrations, participants argued, this was protest done the right way. The American way:
with permits, class, and civility. One slogan in particular became emblematic of all the critics' expectations and fears: "If Hillary Had Won,
We'd Be At Brunch Right Now." The sentiment is surprising only in its
honesty, admitted in public without shame: that Hillary's loss meant more
than the untold losses to come under the sign of Trump. If America—violent, racist America—had elected to its highest seat someone white and
female, the statement implies, approximately zero fucks would be given
for yet another eight years to come.

It makes sense that the template for political movement gone digital
would be black, feminist, and queer. Though strange to say now, after
the election of a supreme leader who delegates the work of fascist pro-
pagandizing to Twitter, Inc., radical politics once found an ally in social
media. Those marginalized in some way by the state—as a matter of race,
gender, sexuality, class, borders, ability—discovered the grand insurgency
within social networks designed above all to communicate information
far and wide with all due speed. Like pamphlets and leaflets, like protective whisper networks and person-to-person rumor mills, like the salon,

the church, the community rec room, the Last Poets' Corner, social media became a space for regular people to deliver all types of information, to congregate and have urgent conversations, to come up with solutions and spread the word to those who need know. After five white women and one brown woman acquitted the murderer George Zimmerman, the world was introduced to a hashtag and a rallying cry that forever changed the course of the internet: Black Lives Matter. But before Black Lives Matter made the hashtag infamous, there was the digital undercommons. In messy but no less meaningful spaces, black people at the intersection of any number of encounters with oppressive powers "talked it out" and developed a language for truth and living.

I was only a little late to having a seat at the table, or more like a seat a couple feet back, scooching closer bit by bit while carrying on my own side conversations and also, mostly, rambling to myself. I found Tumblr near the end of college. I'd had a Twitter account since 2008 and a Facebook account since roughly the same time, but neither matched the unabashed multimedia volume of Tumblr. Twitter, not yet the giant it would become, was the place to mention a sandwich eaten for lunch—not (yet) to elaborately describe it or start a debate over the proper condiments or tag where it came from #spon-style, just to note the fact of a sandwich that was eaten. Facebook, only slightly more evolved, documented vacations and nights out, job offers, law school acceptances, births, deaths, and all those highlights in between. Tumblr was different. It reminded me of the social internet I'd grown up with, online forums where users composed a self-contained identity behind safely anonymous personas like BackstreetGurl220 or CuT773. And this was how I chose to live on Tumblr, behind a blog whose name changed often enough, not unlike those early days on AOL or the various fan sites I frequented in adolescence.

How I found my people I'll never recall for sure, but soon enough my feed was a regular bulletin on the state of affairs, intermixed with memes, photos of Beyoncé and Rihanna, and gifs from Harry Potter or the Marvel Cinematic Universe or some Tumblr cult favorite like Supernatural or Doctor Who that I still haven't ever seen. I was eager to join whatever conversation, to put my three-odd years of literature courses to good use.

My many blog entries, adapted to Tumblr's minimalist lower-case vernacular, were so often bent on righting some pervasive mythology: the crucial delineation between Northerners and abolitionists in the nineteenth
century (the former considered the latter terrorists), William Lloyd Gar-
rison's exploitative relationship with Frederick Douglass (elaborated in the
second of Douglass's three autobiographies, *My Bondage and My Freedom*),
and novels outside public school curricula that could texture the district's
yearly goes at *To Kill a Mockingbird*, such as *The Marrow of Tradition*, *Their
Eyes Were Watching God*, and *The White Boy Shuffle*.

Things moved slower then, or perhaps there was just more room to
sustain a thought. Between my text posts with next to zero likes and even
fewer shares, between the gifs and fan art and stan worship, I learned. I
felt the expanse of diaspora. I learned queer theory well before it entered
any classroom I was privy to, which wouldn't be until graduate school.
I learned about womanism, the black-women-centered praxis coined by
Alice Walker that my graduate courses never mentioned. I learned the
strength and limits of an analytic like Peggy McIntosh's "privilege," via
blogs like thisisthinprivilege, which was excellent at making visible some
axes of power (fatphobia, ableism) while obscuring others (whiteness,
wealth). I was introduced to work by writers and thinkers who taught the
internet how to talk about race, gender, sexuality, and class (for better,
for worse).

While it felt like a haven to me, little reach that I had, I remember the
growing roar, from the many voices who resented any pull toward education and reparation on these matters. No internet platform has ever been
wholly safe for the non-white, non-men, non-straight, non-American;
nowhere on Earth is. The warm-up to the misogynist harassment campaign known as Gamergate, users in the earlier days of social media bore
an onslaught of slurs, death threats, and doxxing attempts on a regular basis with little to no attention from support staff. Contrary to Tumblr's reputation as a social justice oasis, the site with hundreds of millions of blogs
catered to users at all points on the political spectrum with various levels
of willingness to consider the personhood of all people. This was well
before platforms at least pretended to have some sort of contingency plan

for violent-minded white supremacists, trans-exclusionists, and misogynists, eons prior to the federal government's interest in how these groups exposed the pressure points of the civil democracy America holds so dear.

Even within communities connected by shared politics, conflict arose viciously. In a dynamic familiar to anyone who knows a thing or two about how political attachments maintain themselves, online users will vehemently defend their oppressed position while failing to find purchase in someone else's analysis of power. Straight people of color shun queer people of color in pursuit of racial justice. White LGBT blogs omit people of color. Nonblack users talk antiracism and spread antiblackness in the same breath. Trans-exclusionary so-called radical feminists. White worshippers of Susan B. Anthony, similarly uninterested in gender equality for anyone who isn't white or, worse, actively hostile to the barest suggestion that the problems plaguing women of color ought to be included in the wider feminist agenda.

One male feminist gave himself up in the late summer of 2013. Hugo Schwyzer, media darling and prominent women's studies professor at Pasadena City College, was ready to disclose his own fraudulence. Years after he admitted he had preyed on female students and attempted to murder his ex, Schwyzer tweeted that he'd, too, conned his way into his position as a foremost expert on feminism and masculinity. (His educational background is in medieval history.) The admission was an extension of the con, for feminists and womanists had said about as much about Schwyzer for years. Schwyzer apologized to his *Guardian* colleagues Jessica Valenti and Jill Filipovic, "who couldn't work with me or bring themselves to denounce me," as he tweeted, along with "the women of color I trashed in 2008." He added, "I was awful to you because you were in the way." Days later, writer Mikki Kendall, one of the early critics of Schwyzer, tweeted, "#SolidaryIsForWhiteWomen when your concept of feminist history starts & ends with middle class white women. Not the WOC doing the work."

Many women of color who operated within what would later be called online activism circles already knew about Schwyzer, having been the targets of his "trash[ing]" (or, more frankly, harassment) all along.

But not until his clearly stated admission of guilt did his distinguished peers look at him sideways. His apologies were telling. Perhaps inadvertently, Schwyzer revealed that the prolonged silence from well-known, overwhelmingly white, voices in feminist media was not accidental. "For white feminists to enable him for so long is especially galling," Kendall wrote in an essay for Schwyzer's former employer.[1] The hashtag was born out of "frustration intended to be Twitter shorthand for how often feminists of color are told that the racism they experience 'isn't a feminist issue,'" she said.[2]

Schwyzer and his coterie of enablers were the catalyst, the relevant but not isolated case of certain women doubting other women until all is vetted by a white man. Kendall's tag soon grew into something bigger. "#SolidarityIsForWhiteWomen when Woman Is The Nigger of The World is feminist, but actual black women are being divisive for objecting," she tweeted, referencing the Yoko Ono refrain that continues to make the rounds among feminist demonstrations. As others joined in, the hashtag gathered case after case, stories from the workplace, the classroom, out in public, on the historical record. It trended worldwide, attracting the attention of media, including NPR producers, one of whom, ironically, invited Filipovic to comment on the hashtag but not the woman who had coined it.* The tag became, indeed, shorthand for how some feminists continue to politick for a race-forward feminism preoccupied with white—and often affluent—women's lives. "#SolidarityIsForWhiteWomen when you care more about the organic label on your strawberry than about the immigrant woman who harvested it," tweeted the reporter Aura Bogado. "When white women are called brilliant for exposing oppression and women of color are labeled angry. #solidarityisforwhitewomen," tweeted the educational policy professor Patricia D. López.

Schwyzer weighed in soon enough. "This whole #solidarityisfor whitewomen thing is an abusive cudgel to be used against a lot of people who are really working at inclusivity," he tweeted.

---

*NPR later apologized and corrected this mistake ("Twitter, Feminism and Race: Who Gets a Seat at the Table?," *Code Switch*, NPR, September 5, 2013).

Kendall's hashtag rippled across the internet. Another tag, #BlackPower IsForBlackMen, popped up on its heels, similarly listing the ways black women are left out of black political futures that only envision liberation for (straight) men. Not long thereafter, writer and activist Suey Park started #NotYourAsianSideKick to expose expectations in Asian American spaces in an effort to make room for another kind of identity.* Journalists Rania Khalek and Roqayah Chamseddine created #NotYourNarrative to interrogate coverage of the Middle East and North Africa in Western media, coverage so often indicative of the absence of journalists who know the politics and cultures of these regions intimately. Author Janet Mock's #GirlsLikeUs anchored discussions about trans girl- and womanhood and analyst Zerlina Maxwell's #RapeCultureIsWhen tracked the routine behaviors that contribute to violations of consent leading up to and including rape. The hashtag YouOKSis, by author Feminista Jones, combined discussion and action, advocating for humane intervention for victims of street harassment and domestic abuse. Years later, #OscarsSoWhite, created by a marketing director named April Reign, would capture the attention of Hollywood, sparking an industrywide evaluation of the academy's race problem. The academy would again come under scrutiny with #MeToo and #TimesUp campaigns that tapped into the power of a hashtivism once derided, now empowered.

The roots of hashtag activism began several years earlier. The young life of Twitter is segmented by protests and political movements that have made use of its capacity for networks, including the Egyptian revolution and America's Occupy, both in 2011. However, years before #SolidarityIsForWhiteWomen, the limits of hashtag collectivity were starting to appear. In 2012 an organization called Invisible Children, Inc., threw the internet into a frenzy over a single-minded mission to "Stop Kony," a fugitive from the International Criminal Court. The very presidential #Kony2012 campaign succeeded in racking up over one hundred million views for Invisible Children's short documentary and millions of

---

*In 2014 Park tweeted #CancelColbert in response to a tweet by *The Colbert Report* making light of anti-Asian stereotypes. The tweet trended, attracting national attention along with threats of violence that drove Park to move out of her Chicago home.

dollars in donations, the majority of which may have been fed back into marketing, salaries, and filmmaking costs, according to a published account of its 2011 expenses.* #Kony2012 also transformed a war criminal into a meme and emboldened US military involvement in Africa, despite dissent from Ugandan grassroots organizations.†

But sentimentality was not exactly the object of critique when hashtag activism amassed enough momentum to become legible enough to decry. The old guard wasn't pleased. The loudest and most venerated opinions were usually not from veteran activists, but from the usual pundits who made snide comments about the ease of the work. Though their skepticism made little sense in the context of homegrown slogans whose purpose was merely to start a conversation, such as #NotYourAsianSidekick, or to include actionable follow-through, such as #YouOKSis, popular criticism conflated long-working organizers with the retweet button as part of the kit and caboodle that is the "wussification of America," to borrow from former Pennsylvania governor Ed Rendell and Fox News.‡ The blue-hairs argued that, like Seamless and Netflix and all the cultural staples we millennials have reportedly "killed" (not limited to napkins, handshakes, sex, and Big Macs), hashtag activism evinces again our aversion to effort and labor—never mind that we are the generation working harder and longer for less pay than our parents and grandparents.

The argument was never about work. The talking head or regular columnist or incumbent politician in his cushy gig isn't offended by the

---

* In 2012 Invisible Children's director of ideology—yes!—told *Good* magazine that 63 percent of their budget went towards salaries, overheads, and "awareness programs" (Cord Jefferson, "'There's a Rabid Hunger to Criticize': A 'Kony 2012' Creator Defends the Film," *Good*, March 10, 2012).

† A few years later, another hashtag, #BringBackOurGirls, sparked by a mass kidnapping by the rebel group Boko Haram in Chibok, Uganda, would again highlight the link between Western attention and reparative action. Author Teju Cole criticized its sensationalism, tweeting in May 2014, "Remember: #bringbackourgirls, a vital moment for Nigerian democracy, is not the same as #bringbackourgirls, a wave of global sentimentality."

‡ In 2016, activists in Chicago successfully ousted Cook County's state's attorney, Anita Alvarez, with the "Bye, Anita" (#ByeAnita) campaign. It was provoked by Alvarez's delayed response to Officer Jason Van Dyke shooting Laquan McDonald sixteen times and killing the black teen.

effort, or perceived lack thereof—he is offended by the project, the very pursuit of some kind of justice in this country. The advent of Black Lives Matter, a statement, a motto, a chant, an ethos, laid everything on the table. Black Lives Matter unmasked everyone's prejudices, on either side of the liberal-conservative divide. All the romance America believes about revolution and protest, from the Founding Fathers to the strung-out likenesses of civil rights leaders insisted upon by educators and politicians, collapsed like wet toilet paper. "Black Lives Matter," the simple, chaste affirmation that black people deserve life, was enough to make America lose every fiber of its mind. Until, that is, the rest of America needed a template for organizing in the new millennium.

Organizers Alicia Garza, Patrisse Cullors, and Opal Tometi created #BlackLivesMatter in 2013 in response to the acquittal of George Zimmerman, who murdered teenage Trayvon Martin in 2012. They did so during the media circus that put a dead black boy on trial for his own death, a routine to be repeated with Michael Brown and any other black person pronounced dead by passive voice.* This was not the usual case of an openly racist Fox News, doing what it does best, but the as-regular racism of progressive media entities. "Trayvon Martin did, in fact, cause his own death," Zimmerman's lead defense attorney, Mark O'Mara, concluded in July 2013. "Michael Brown, 18, due to be buried on Monday, was no angel," the *New York Times*' John Eligon reported on August 2014.[3]

It was following Darren Wilson's lethal action that #BlackLivesMatter found its movement, coinciding with weeks and months of protests as the bureau of Ferguson not only failed to reckon with its injustices, but smeared the stain of violence, firing tear gas and rubber bullets into protesters at will from atop armored vehicles. Police were hurting people. SWAT was hurting people. Journalists were threatened with violence for

---

*"The list of nonindictments in the wake of state murders of Black people continues to grow: Michael Brown, John Crawford, Aiyana Stanley-Jones, Sandra Bland, Jonathan Ferrell, Miriam Carey, Tamir Rice, Rekia Boyd," Christina Sharpe writes in *In the Wake: On Blackness and Being.* "Black being appears in the space of the asterisked human as the insurance for, as that which underwrites, white circulation as the human."

reporting what they saw, and then were assaulted anyway. A man was quoted calling it a "war zone," the parallels between America's hatred for darker peoples abroad and at home, again and always, undeniable.

Black Lives Matter made social media crucial and informative. Meeting spots and actions and funds were drawn up between strangers. Expressions of solidarity reached across the globe to and from Palestine, the United Kingdom, and France. Marches narrated in the moment contradicted the national news outlets that were too concerned with impressing white moderates to speak freely about what was happening. This all despite enormous pushback from social media platforms themselves. Twitter, whose executives once bragged about the power of free speech, acquired the live-streaming app Periscope in 2015 and afterward began censoring videos that showed police violence. Facebook adopted similar measures.

As police continue to kill people, #BlackLivesMatter remains in the air, a sickly symbiotic relationship that's become a normal fact of online life. Digital and oh so visible, it was inevitable that the phrase would reach meme status, subject to all the appropriations and mutations that haunt blackness gone viral. In the 1970s, the white working class fell into a pit it called "the blue-collar blues," a depression caused by a black upward mobility they perceived had outpaced their own—yet, still needed use of black aesthetics to articulate itself. In the new millennium, there is All Lives Matter and the more absurd Blue Lives Matter, anti-black counter-slogans that nonetheless cannot escape the rhetorical world black people made. Indeed, as scholars P. Khalil Saucier and Tryon P. Woods have observed, "The meme has become a political Rorschach producing a cornucopia of identitarian hashtags . . . that, at the end of the day, effortlessly obscures or subsumes blackness's grammar of suffering."[4] Walking past the local doggy daycare, I saw a sign that read "Beagle Lives Matter" in white on black text. I took a picture. A few weeks later, the sign was gone. In 2017 a nonblack high-schooler tweeted his acceptance letter to Stanford University along with his application essay. The document read "#BlackLivesMatter" one hundred times in a row. (Did he type it or relegate the work to copy and paste?) The prompt was "What matters to you, and why?"

The lead-up to the 2016 presidential election was bizarre and so, so American. As the soon-to-be-president of the United States of America ran on a platform of white supremacy, white liberals made jokes and entreated brown and black people to comport themselves a little more respectably. Anger and our exhaustion was repugnant. "Smile," they said. "We're about to have a woman president." And then white people elected Trump.

In the wake, in the grasping, it was amazing to see what those optimists reached for. The word "self-care" surged as affluent women lost themselves in expensive skincare routines. When, in the epilogue of her 1988 essay collection, *A Burst of Light*, Audre Lorde, tending to her black, ailing body in the late stages of cancer, asserts that caring for herself is "an act of political warfare," her words dream up a reflexive encounter with oneself protected from the limitations of societal custom.[5] *This day* takes this black, ailing woman's words as reason to reify consumer impulses, from nail services provided by underpaid technicians to step-by-step fitness routines to must-have bath bombs, body butters, candles. "It was the new chicken soup for the progressive soul," observed Aisha Harris in a history of the concept on *Slate*.[6] White people aren't the only ones who have taken self-care for a ride, but the market transparently bends to the tastes of white, affluent, nondisabled people.* The politics of self-care on white, affluent, nondisabled bodies looks a lot like the tenor of white optimism that got everyone here in the first place.

Anger, too, experienced a makeover. The most racialized emotion in American history was suddenly *cool*. That hadn't been true before. America fears anger from black people, has always feared anger from black people, considers black people angry even when something more like "despaired" or "fatigued" better suits the mood. In the nineteenth century, dissent

---

*How many luxury skin products, in your cabinet and mine, evoke some Indigenous fantasy? Drunk Elephant, its logo modeled after the creature native to sub-Saharan Africa and South Asia, stokes a mythology of the Dark Continent with aplomb. "This Virgin Marula Oil is totally pure, which is the way it is used by African women," the company beckons in one product description, "so close your eyes and pretend you're sitting under a beautiful Marula tree. . . . Skin will never know the difference!"

from the enslaved was diagnosed as a mental illness by physicians. "Drap-etomania" and "dysaethesia aethiopica," characterized by "mischief" and "troublesome" conduct, turned a desire to be free into a form of madness. In the mid-twentieth century, the diagnostic criteria for schizophrenia transformed from a benign affliction found often among middle-class white women to an illness characterized by volatility and associated with black people, particularly black men. "Many leading medical and popular sources suddenly described schizophrenia as an illness manifested not by docility, but rage," psychiatrist and scholar Jonathan M. Metzl found in his study *The Protest Psychosis*.[7] The book's title comes from an article published in 1968 in the *Archives of General Psychiatry* whose authors, the noted psychiatrists Walter Bromberg and Frank Simon, called schizophrenia a "protest psychosis" shared among young American Negroes. "In the worst cases," writes Metzl, "psychiatric authors conflated the schizophrenic symptoms of African American patients with the perceived schizophrenia of civil rights protests."[8]

After years or perhaps decades or perhaps centuries of slights and rules of etiquette, anger and outrage has become the mood du jour. It is mainstream to embrace the spirit of the harpy. Like a valve left closed since the start of the '80s, now open again, it is okay to admit to feeling angry about the state of the nation. Rage is all the rage. After Ferguson, after Baltimore, after Chicago, after Oakland, everyone can march and make a hashtag and be proud and mad and make it home safely. As long as well-heeled white people are angry, others can be angry too.*

Anger is not a privilege. Anger expressed in public is a privilege. Anger expressed in public and left in public is a privilege. Anger picked up and dropped off like dry cleaning. Anger learned from dystopian fiction and not dystopian reality. Anger neutralized by the hope that the pendulum must eventually swing the other way. Anger neutralized by the knowledge

---

*Or perhaps not. On the weekend of July 14, 2018, Chicago police escalated violence against black demonstrators who gathered after police shot and killed thirty-seven-year-old Harith Augustus, who was described as "exhibiting characteristics of an armed person." Just a week prior, state police cheerfully acquiesced to an anti-gun-violence march down the Dan Ryan Expressway led by white celebrity priest Father Michael Pfleger.

that the other end of the pendulum's arc means opportunity and thriving. Anger neutralized by faith in what American has been and can be. Anger chosen like a chalky vitamin, not in-born like bile. But anger, deserved and glorious anger, cannot feed the soul. Anger is the one who feeds.

A protest is not an event but an endurance test. If we survive, it's only for sharing such a scourge.

I hope everyone keeps on till tomorrow, whenever that comes.

Business as Usual

"Come on up, Dr. Miller," called Evans from the head
of the stairs. "There's time enough, but none to spare."

In an essay published by the *Chronicle of Higher Education* in 2017, literary theorist Walter Benn Michaels argues against the existence of cultural appropriation, calling it, per the essay's title, a "myth." His reasoning does not begin with his disbelief in the ordering power of racism—a position netting him a fair amount of notoriety within and outside academia—but with his disbelief in the existence of culture, period. "The problem is that the whole idea of cultural identity is incoherent," he writes, too incoherent to draw lines around, too slippery to hold, too capricious, too rhetorical to lay any sort of meaningful claim to.[1] Naming several of the prestigious greatest hits of the great appropriation wars—Dana Schutz, "Kenny" Goldsmith, Sam Durant, and, *well*, AncestryDNA—Michaels believes it was false propriety and fictive kinship, not racial science or anti-blackness or bad art, that "got them in trouble."[*] Even if white privilege "enabled them to treat something that didn't belong to them as if it did," that quandary can only be a quandary if another kind of privilege, genetics, enables people of color to treat something, culture, that does not belong to them as if it does. In short, investment in cultural difference gives appropriation life, Michaels says, lobbing the ball back across the net.

I don't wholly disagree with Michaels—culture *is* incoherent and confusing and borderless just as much as it is shared and trenchant and guarded

---

[*] "Trouble" here seems to mean embarrassment and a few impassioned opinion pieces.

and intuited. The same way that I share language and traditions with white friends who also grew up in the Midwest and have stayed in the Midwest, I have language and traditions that they don't share, that I better share with strangers who are black and grew up in the South, in England, in the West Indies, or in Canada. And they, too, have language and traditions better shared with others around them, of whatever race, than with a black American from the Midwest. Culture is contradictory, not mythical.

Lost in an elaborate whodunit, Michaels (along with less intelligent critics) deeply misreads the terms of grievance, pinning the propriety impulses on the language of the oppressed. However, the initial ownership claim is not made by the person who notices the disparity between who labors and who profits, but by the entity who declares the right to claim and profit in the first place. "No stories belong to anyone," may be true in spirit—in law and capital it is quite another matter. Ideas and practices and art and appearances accrue value the whiter they become, the whiter they are perceived as being all along. Underwriting is a money matter. And black people have been underwriting white capital for centuries.

Binding the disparate cultural touchstones in this book, appropriation runs on desire more than hatred, inattention more than intention. I've made my case out of cases, making the commonplace exceptional by default, but I cannot overstate the regularity of appropriation, how often it is, for most, a nondilemma. Appropriation is impossible to delaminate from our most basic appreciation of what it means to create and share something, whether or not that something was ever intended to be for sale. Appropriative gestures are devilish in their contortions, every bit as convoluted as they make you feel by sussing them out.

Complex problems often deserve complex solutions, but in the case of power and appropriation the answer is quite simple when looked at from a bird's-eye view. Equality is too tame. Fair compensation is too modest. Our world deserves reordering. Only under a transformation on that scale could I ever imagine a version of society in which black people have options instead of destinies, options instead of statistics. Reorganizing the terms of what counts and who counts on planet Earth and beyond is only fathomable by minds more creative than my own.

At a humbler level, in the here and now and the everyday, we are alone together with our desires and our gestures. We are all of us tainted by the forces that order our world—capitalism, anti-blackness, imperialism—and saying so is not the same as license to roll over and accept come what may. On the contrary, if there is a call embedded in this book—and even at this stage, I am not sure if there is—it is a call to more alertness, more intensity, more care, and more fluency in the racial dramas performed as part and parcel of business as usual. "There's time enough, but none to spare."

There is time enough, but none to spare.

ACKNOWLEDGMENTS

To Jorge Cotte, my biggest supporter and confidant, I am so, so thankful you are you.

To my agent, William Callahan, who saw this book before I wrote a single word of it.

To my editor, Rakia Clark, this project's fierce champion, thank you for your faith and ferocity.

To the team at Beacon Press, thank you for bringing this book to life. Thank you, Kate Scott and Susan Lumenello, for keeping up with the nitty-gritty of all the vernacular worlds this book brings together. Thank you, Louis Roe, for the sly cover.

To my dissertation committee, whose patience and guidance make the difficult questions irresistible, whatever format my inquiry takes. To Lauren Berlant, thank you for your brilliance and care, thank you for the gift enabling me to take my work as seriously as you always have. To Adrienne Brown, thank you for your keen eye and attention to the shallows and the gaps.

To the editors across the real-life internet who let me wade in ambivalence, the place so formative to the writing in this book. To Matt Buchanan, David A. Graham, and Malcolm Harris, the first editors who took a chance on me and taught me how to tell stories with criticism. To Julie Beck, Shanley Kane, Alexandra Molotkow, and Sandra Song for making room for aesthetics in technology coverage. To Melvin Backman, Maya Binyam, Gazelle Emami, Sam Hockley-Smith, Brendan Klinkenberg, Ezekiel Kweku, and Tomi Obaro for the space to think about racial performance as things are, without shortcuts.

To my peers turned best friends, who've celebrated my wins like their own. To Brandon Truett and Jacob Harris, thank you for solidarity and a true lifeline in gossip.

To my family—thank you to my parents, Michele and Tom Shippy, who will, in my mother's words, "know you have a book in you" enough times throughout your life that you'll start to believe it. Thank you to my brother, John, for always going with the flow.

NOTES

INTRODUCTION: APPROPRIATION AND AMERICAN MYTHMAKING

1. All epigraphs are from Charles W. Chesnutt, *The Marrow of Tradition* (1901), ed. Werner Sollors (New York: W. W. Norton, 2012).

2. Langston Hughes, "Note on Commercial Theatre," in *The Norton Anthology of American Literature*, 9th ed., ed. Robert S. Levine, vol. 2 (New York: W. W. Norton, 2017).

3. Hughes, "Note on Commercial Theatre."

4. Adam Bernard, "Grandmaster Caz Interview," RapReviews.com, March 7, 2007, http://www.rapreviews.com/interview/caz2007.html.

5. "Cultural Appropriation: A Roundtable," *Artforum*, Summer 2017.

6. Lauren Berlant, "Cruel Optimism," in *The Affect Theory Reader*, ed. Melissa Gregg and Gregory J. Seigworth (Durham, NC: Duke University Press, 2010).

7. William Darity Jr. et al., *What We Get Wrong About Closing the Racial Wealth Gap* (Durham, NC: Samuel DuBois Cook Center on Social Equity/Insight Center for Community Economic Development, 2018).

8. Chuck Collins et al., *The Ever-Growing Gap: Without Change, African-American and Latino Families Won't Match White Wealth for Centuries* (Washington, DC: Institute for Policy Studies, 2016).

CHAPTER 1: THE POP STAR

1. Austin Scaggs, "Christina Aguilera: Dirty Girl Cleans Up," *Rolling Stone*, August 24, 2006, https://www.rollingstone.com/music/music-features/christina-aguilera-dirty-girl-cleans-up-108302.

2. Lynn Hirschberg, "From the Vaults: The Fall & Rise of Christina Aguilera," *W*, July 2011, https://www.wmagazine.com/story/christina-aguilera-cover-story.

3. Hirschberg, "From the Vaults."

4. LeRoi Jones, *Blues People: Negro Music in White America* (New York: William Morrow, 1963).

5. John Jeremiah Sullivan, "The Curses: Part I," *Sewanee Review* (Winter 2017), https://thesewaneereview.com/articles/the-curses.

6. Sullivan, "The Curses: Part I."

7. Lester Bangs, *Psychotic Reactions and Carburetor Dung,* ed. Greil Marcus (New York: Anchor Books, 1987).

8. Bruce Springsteen, *Songs* (New York: HarperCollins, 2003).

9. Jefferson Cowie, *Stayin' Alive: The 1970s and the Last Days of the Working Class* (New York: New Press, 2010).

10. Josh Kun, "Christina Aguilera, 'Stripped' (RCA)," review of *Stripped,* by Christina Aguilera, *Spin,* July 15, 2003, https://www.spin.com/2003/07/christina-aguilera-stripped-rca.

11. "Christina Aguilera Addresses 'Not Latina Enough' Criticism, Opens Up About Her Hispanic Heritage and Estranged Father," *Huffington Post,* Latino Voices, February 7, 2012, https://www.huffingtonpost.com/2012/02/07/christina-aguilera-_n_1258067.html.

12. Neil Strauss, "Christina Aguilera: The Hit Girl," *Rolling Stone,* July 6, 2000, https://www.rollingstone.com/music/music-features/christina-aguilera-the-hit-girl-190789.

13. Kim Stitzel, "Not Your Puppet," *MTV,* February 28, 2002, http://www.mtv.com/bands/a/aguilera_christina/news_feature_feb_02.

14. Jancee Dunn, review of *Stripped,* by Christina Aguilera, *Rolling Stone,* November 5, 2002.

15. Kun, "Christina Aguilera."

16. bell hooks, "Eating the Other: Desire and Resistance," in *Black Looks: Race and Representation* (Boston: South End Press, 1992).

17. "Ending Violence against Native Women," Indian Law Resource Center, https://indianlaw.org/issue/ending-violence-against-native-women, accessed April 25, 2019.

18. Hilton Als, "You and Whose Army?," in *White Girls* (San Francisco: McSweeney's, 2013).

19. hooks, "Eating the Other."

20. hooks, "Eating the Other."

21. Evelyn Wang, "Here's Why Adam Wiles Named Himself Calvin Harris," *Esquire,* June 2, 2016, https://www.esquire.com/entertainment/news/a45441/calvin-harris-name-why.

22. Brooks Barnes, "Revealing Photo Threatens a Major Disney Franchise," *New York Times,* April 28, 2008, https://www.nytimes.com/2008/04/28/business/media/28hannah.html.

23. Todd Venezia, "Disney 'to Cast Aside Nude Photo Actress Miley Cyrus,'" *Daily Telegraph,* May 1, 2008, archived at Wayback Machine, https://web.archive.org/web/20080501111923.

24. Barnes, "Revealing Photo Threatens a Major Disney Franchise."

25. Bruce Handy, "Miley Knows Best," *Vanity Fair,* June 2008, https://www.vanityfair.com/culture/2008/06/miley200806.

26. "Christina Aguilera Has Recorded a New Song, but It's Not for Her Upcoming Album," *MTV News,* July 5, 2004, archived at Wayback Machine, https://web.archive.org/web/20130921081929.

27. Lola Ogunnaike, "Christina Aguilera, That Dirrty Girl, Cleans Up Real Nice," *New York Times,* July 30, 2006, https://www.nytimes.com/2006/07/30/arts/30ogun.html.

28. Ogunnaike, "That Dirrty Girl, Cleans Up Real Nice."

29. Ogunnaike, "That Dirrty Girl, Cleans Up Real Nice."

30. Sasha Frere-Jones, "Sex Symbols," *New Yorker*, September 4, 2006, https://www.newyorker.com/magazine/2006/09/04/sex-symbols.

31. Frere-Jones, "Sex Symbols."

32. Evelyn Wang, "Here's Why Adam Wiles Named Himself Calvin Harris," *Esquire*, June 2, 2016, "Christina Aguilera."

CHAPTER 2: THE COVER GIRL

1. Lee Wohlfert, "When Disco Queen Grace Jones Lamented 'I Need a Man,' Artist Jean-Paul Goude Prowled Too Near Her Cage," *People*, April 23, 1979, https://people.com/archive/when-disco-queen-grace-jones-lamented-i-need-a-man-artist-jean-paul-goude-prowled-too-near-her-cage-vol-11-no-16.

2. Kathleen Hou, "Marc Jacobs Models Wore Dreadlocks from Etsy," *New York*, September 15, 2016.

3. Hou, "Marc Jacobs Models Wore Dreadlocks from Etsy."

4. Eric Wilson, "Marc Jacobs on Hip Hop and Charges of Cultural Appropriation: 'Maybe I've Been Insensitive,'" *InStyle*, August 7, 2017, https://www.instyle.com/fashion/marc-jacobs-hip-hop-icons.

5. Ellie Krupnick, "What That Famous 'Devil Wears Prada' Scene Actually Gets Wrong," *Huffington Post*, January 24, 2014, https://www.huffpost.com/entry/devil-wears-prada-scene-famous_n_4659819.

6. Katherine Rosman, "The Itsy-Bitsy, Teenie-Weenie, Very Litigious Bikini," *New York Times*, December 20, 2018, https://www.nytimes.com/2018/12/20/business/kiini-bikini-lawsuit-ipek-irgit-solange-ferrarini.html.

7. Sarah Mower, "Spring 2016 Ready-to-Wear: Valentino," *Vogue*, October 6, 2015, https://www.vogue.com/fashion-shows/spring-2016-ready-to-wear/valentino.

8. Dana Oliver, "These Are Bantu Knots, Not 'Mini Buns.' There's a Difference," *Huffington Post*, May 28, 2015, https://www.huffpost.com/entry/bantu-knots-mini-buns-difference_n_7452532.

9. Hilton Als, "The Only One," in Als, *White Girls*.

10. Kristina Rodulfo, "Everything We Know About Beauty We Learned from Drag Queens," *Elle*, December 11, 2018, https://www.elle.com/beauty/makeup-skin-care/a25426378/drag-influence-beauty-industry.

11. Rodulfo, "Everything We Know About Beauty We Learned from Drag Queens."

CHAPTER 3: THE ARTIST

1. Jeff Selle and Maureen Dolan, "Black Like Me? Civil Rights Activist's Ethnicity Questioned," *Coeur d'Alene Press*, June 11, 2015, https://www.cdapress.com/archive/article-385adfeb-76f3-5050-98b4-d4bf021c423f.html.

2. Ijeoma Oluo, "The Heart of Whiteness: Ijeoma Oluo Interviews Rachel Dolezal, the White Woman Who Identifies as Black," *Stranger*, April 19, 2017, https://www.thestranger.com/features/2017/04/19/25082450/the-heart-of-whiteness-ijeoma-oluo-interviews-rachel-dolezal-the-white-woman-who-identifies-as-black.

3. Rachel Dolezal, *In Full Color: Finding My Place in a Black and White World* (Dallas: BenBella Books, 2017).

4. Eunsong Kim and Maya Isabella Mackrandilal, "The Whitney Biennial for Angry Women," *New Inquiry*, April 4, 2014, https://thenewinquiry.com/the-whitney -biennial-for-angry-women.

5. Whitney Museum of Art, *Whitney Biennial*, 2014 brochure, quoted in Jessica Valenti, "Art, Gender and Pleasure Should Collide More Often—Just Like on the Clit Rodeo," *Guardian*, May 16, 2014, https://www.theguardian.com/commentis free/2014/may/16/art-gender-artist-sophia-wallace-interview.

6. Kim and Mackrandilal, "The Whitney Biennial for Angry Women."

7. Jeremy Sigler, "Joe Scanlan," *BOMB*, July 1, 2010, https://bombmagazine.org /articles/joe-scanlan.

8. Sigler, "Joe Scanlan."

9. Andrew Russeth, "There's Something Funny About Donelle Woolford," *Observer*, March 3, 2014, https://observer.com/2014/03/theres-something-funny-about -donelle-woolford.

10. Carolina A. Miranda, "Art and Race at the Whitney: Rethinking the Donelle Woolford Debate," *Los Angeles Times*, July 17, 2014.

11. Miranda, "Art and Race at the Whitney."

12. Jennifer Kidwell, "Performance and Para-Fiction: Jennifer Kidwell on Playing Donelle Woolford," *Hyperallergic*, December 23, 2014, https://hyperallergic .com/170408/performance-and-para-fiction-jennifer-kidwell-on-playing-donelle -woolford.

13. Kidwell, "Performance and Para-Fiction."

14. Kenneth Goldsmith, "It's Not Plagiarism. In the Digital Age, It's 'Repurposing,'" *Chronicle of Higher Education*, September 11, 2011, https://www.chronicle .com/article/Uncreative-Writing/128908.

15. Alec Wilkinson, "Something Borrowed," *New Yorker*, October 5, 2015, https:// www.newyorker.com/magazine/2015/10/05/something-borrowed-wilkinson.

16. Jillian Steinhauer, "Kenneth Goldsmith Remixes Michael Brown Autopsy Report as Poetry," *Hyperallergic*, March 16, 2015, https://hyperallergic.com/190954 /kenneth-goldsmith-remixes-michael-brown-autopsy-report-as-poetry.

17. Wilkinson, "Something Borrowed."

18. Ajay Kurian, "The Ballet of White Victimhood: On Jordan Wolfson, Petroushka, and Donald Trump," *Artspace*, November 15, 2016, https://www.artspace .com/magazine/contributors/jottings/ajay-kurian-on-jordan-wolfson-colored -sculpture-54364.

19. Hrag Vartanian, "The Violence of the 2017 Whitney Biennial," *Hyperallergic*, March 20, 2017, https://hyperallergic.com/366688/the-violence-of-the-2017 -whitney-biennial.

20. Lizzie Crocker, "Protesters Want This Painting of Emmett Till Destroyed—Because the Artist Is White," *Daily Beast*, March 21, 2017, https://www.thedaily beast.com/protesters-want-this-painting-of-emmett-till-destroyedbecause-the-artist -is-white.

21. Anya Jaremko-Greenwold, "Protesters Block, Demand Removal of a Painting of Emmett Till at the Whitney Biennial," *Hyperallergic*, March 22, 2017, https://

hyperallergic.com/367012/protesters-block-demand-removal-of-a-painting-of
-emmett-till-at-the-whitney-biennial.

CHAPTER 4: THE HIPSTER

1. Katy Steinmetz, "Poll: What Is 2011's Word of the Year?," *Time*, December 7, 2011, http://newsfeed.time.com/2011/12/07/poll-what-is-2011s-word-of-the-year.

2. Katy Steinmetz, "Poll: What Word Should Be Banished in 2012?," *Time*, January 11, 2012, http://newsfeed.time.com/2012/01/11/poll-what-word-should -be-banished-in-2012.

3. Katy Steinmetz, "Poll: What Word Should Be Banished in 2013?," *Time*, December 26, 2012, http://newsfeed.time.com/2012/12/26/poll-what-word-should -be-banished-in-2013.

4. Katy Steinmetz, "Which Word Should Be Banned in 2015?," *Time*, November 12, 2014, http://time.com/3576870/worst-words-poll-2014.

5. Lake Superior State University (LSSU), "Banished Word List Archive," 2015. Links for specific years at www.lssu.edu/banished-words-list/banished-word-list -archive.

6. LSSU, "Banished Word List Archive," 2015.

7. LSSU, "Banished Word List Archive," 2015.

8. LSSU, "Banished Word List Archive," 2016.

9. " 'Bigly,' 'Dadbod,' 'Post-truth' Make 2016 List of Banished Words," *Chicago Tribune*, December 31, 2016, https://www.chicagotribune.com/news/nationworld /ct-banned-words-20161231-story.html.

10. LSSU, "Banished Word List Archive," 2017; LSSU, "Banished Word List Archive," 2018.

11. Steinmetz, "Which Word Should Be Banned in 2015?"

12. Steinmetz, "Which Word Should Be Banned in 2015?"

13. LSSU, "Banished Word List Archive," 2015.

14. Samantha Allen, "Feminist, Bae, Turnt: Time's 'Worst Words' List Is Sexist and Racist," *Daily Beast*, November 13, 2014, https://www.thedailybeast.com /feminist-bae-turnt-times-worst-words-list-is-sexist-and-racist.

15. LSSU, "Banished Word List Archive," 2004.

16. LSSU, "Banished Word List Archive," 2005.

17. James Baldwin, "If Black English Isn't a Language, Then Tell Me, What Is?" *New York Times*, July 29, 1979, https://archive.nytimes.com/www.nytimes .com/books/98/03/29/specials/baldwin-english.html.

18. Kashana Cauley, "Word: Woke," *Believer*, February 1, 2019, https:// believermag.com/word-woke.

19. Cauley, "Word: Woke."

20. *Oxford English Dictionary*, "Word of the Year 2018: Shortlist," https:// en.oxforddictionaries.com/word-of-the-year/shortlist-2018.

21. Kyrell Grant, "The Inventor of Big Dick Energy on the Rise and Demise of a Horny Twitter Joke," *Broadly*, June 29, 2018, https://broadly.vice.com/en_us /article/pavnn9/the-inventor-of-big-dick-energy-on-twitter-joke.

22. Grant, "The Inventor of Big Dick Energy"; Kyrell Grant, " 'It Sucks, Because I Made Zero Dollars from It': How I Coined Big Dick Energy," *Guardian*,

December 21, 2018, https://www.theguardian.com/culture/2018/dec/21/people-of
-2018-big-dick-energy-buzz-phrase.

23. Grant, "Inventor of Big Dick Energy"; Grant, "It Sucks."

24. Grant, "Inventor of Big Dick Energy."

25. Grant, "Inventor of Big Dick Energy."

26. Norman Mailer, "The White Negro," 1957, *Dissent*, June 20, 2007, https://
www.dissentmagazine.org/online_articles/the-white-negro-fall-1957.

27. Mailer, "The White Negro."

28. Mailer, "The White Negro."

29. Mailer, "The White Negro."

30. Mailer, "The White Negro."

CHAPTER 5: THE MEME

1. Elise Kramer, "The Playful Is Political: The Metapragmatics of Internet
Rape-Joke Arguments," *Language in Society* (April 2011): doi.org/10.1017/S004740
4511000017.

2. Doreen St. Félix, "Black Teens Are Breaking the Internet and Seeing None
of the Profits," *Fader*, December 3, 2015, https://www.thefader.com/2015/12/03
/on-fleek-peaches-monroee-meechie-viral-vines.

3. Jennifer Lynn Stoever, *The Sonic Color Line: Race and the Cultural Politics of
Listening* (New York: New York University Press, 2016). Stoever adapts her concept
from Du Bois's elaboration of the color line in works such as *The Souls of Black Folk*
(1903) and *Dusk of Dawn* (1940).

4. Geneva Smitherman, *Talkin and Testifyin: The Language of Black America* (Detroit: Wayne State University Press, 1977).

5. Jordan Darville, "R.I.P. Vine: Here Are Some of the Best Vines That Ever
Existed," *Fader*, October 27, 2016, https://www.thefader.com/2016/10/27/classic
-vine-list.

6. Casey Newton, "Why Vine Died," *Verge*, October 28, 2016, https://www
.theverge.com/2016/10/28/13456208/why-vine-died-twitter-shutdown.

7. Hannah Giorgis, "Black Users on Vine: Celebrating Blackness 6 Seconds at a
Time," *Guardian*, May 17, 2015, https://www.theguardian.com/commentisfree
/2015/may/17/black-users-on-vine-celebrating-blackness-6-seconds-at-a-time.

8. Taylor Lorenz, "Inside the Secret Meeting That Changed the Fate of Vine
Forever," Mic, October 29, 2016, https://mic.com/articles/157977/inside-the-secret
-meeting-that-changed-the-fate-of-vine-forever#.zWWFgvT1C.

9. Malcolm Harris, *Kids These Days: Human Capital and the Making of Millennials*
(Boston: Little, Brown, 2017).

10. Félix, "Black Teens Are Breaking the Internet."

11. Sydney Gore, "Kayla Newman Launches on Fleek Extensions by Peaches
Monroee," *Fader*, September 2, 2017, https://www.thefader.com/2017/09/02/kayla
-newman-launches-on-fleek-extensions-by-peaches-monroee.

12. Joshua Lumpkin Green, "Digital Blackface: The Repackaging of the Black
Masculine Image," master's thesis, Miami University, 2006, http://rave.ohiolink
.edu/etdc/view?acc_num=miami1154371043.

13. Green, "Digital Blackface."

14. Katherine Brown, "Everyday I'm Tumblin': Performing Online Identity Through Reaction GIFs," master's thesis, School of the Art Institute of Chicago, 2012.

15. Sara Ahmed, "Declarations of Whiteness: The Non-Performativity of Anti-Racism," *borderlands* 3, no. 2 (2006), http://www.borderlands.net.au/vol3no2_2004 /ahmed_declarations.htm.

CHAPTER 6: THE VIRAL STAR

1. "Oklahoma City Apartment Complex Catches Fire, 5 Units Damaged; Sweet Brown Explains," *Oklahoma News 4*, KFOR-TV, April 8, 2012.

2. Stephen Holden, "Brutal, Painful Death, Just a Mouse Click Away," *New York Times*, January 25, 2008, https://www.nytimes.com/2008/01/25/movies/25untr .html; Claudia Puig, "'Untraceable': Don't Bother Looking for It,'" *USA Today*, January 24, 2008, https://usatoday30.usatoday.com/life/movies/reviews/2008-01-24 -untraceable_N.htm.

3. "Apollo Guide," Rotten Tomatoes, www.rottentomatoes.com/source-19, accessed April 26, 2019.

4. Logan Paul Vlogs, *Kong Killed Another Animal . . .* YouTube, December 24, 2017, https://www.youtube.com/watch?v=noJKc7-qfjc.

5. Natalie Robehmed, "How YouTube Star Logan Paul Made $14.5 Million amid Scandal," *Forbes*, December 3, 2018, https://www.forbes.com/sites/natalier-obehmed/2018/12/03/how-youtube-star-logan-paul-made-14-5-million-amid -scandal/#8d3bbba6b2d4.

6. *We Rescued a Baby Duckling!*, YouTube, May 1, 2018, https://www.youtube.com /watch?v=0utqwnvanzg; *Releasing My $10,000 Albino Turtle!*, YouTube, May 20, 2018, https://www.youtube.com/watch?v=serIs70zQzQ.

CHAPTER 7: THE CHEF

1. On the Big House, see "Historic Buildings, the Whitney Plantation," Whitney Plantation (website), www.whitneyplantation.com/education/louisiana-history /the-big-house-and-the-outbuildings, accessed April 24, 2019.

2. Paula Deen and Sherry Suib Cohen, *Paula Deen: It Ain't All About the Cookin'* (New York: Simon & Schuster, 2007).

3. Paula Forbes, "Here's the Racist Paula Deen Deposition Transcript," Eater, June 20, 2013, https://www.eater.com/2013/6/20/6417349/heres-the-racist-paula -deen-deposition-transcript.

4. Forbes, "Here's the Racist Paula Deen Deposition Transcript."

5. Mark Memmott, "Paula Dean Cooks Up $75 Million Deal with Investor," *The Two-Way*, NPR, February 13, 2014, https://www.npr.org/sections/thetwo -way/2014/02/13/276440639/paula-deen-cooks-up-75-million-deal-with-investor.

6. "Projects for Paula Deen's Family Kitchen," Lock & Key Productions, www .lochandkeyproductions.com/client/paula-deens-family-kitchen/, accessed April 25, 2019.

7. Ingela Ratledge, "Anthony Bourdain's Celebrity Chef Smackdown!," *TV Guide*, August 18, 2011, https://www.tvguide.com/news/anthony-bourdains -celebrity-1036482.

8. Kim Severson, "Paula Deen's Cook Tells of Slights, Steeped in History," *New York Times*, July 24, 2013, https://www.nytimes.com/2013/07/25/us/paula-deens-soul-sister-portrays-an-unequal-bond.html.

9. Severson, "Paula Deen's Cook Tells of Slights."

10. Severson, "Paula Deen's Cook Tells of Slights."

11. Chris Furmeister, "'Ugly Delicious' Delves into the Complicated History of an American Staple in 'Fried Chicken,'" Eater, February 23, 2018, https://www.eater.com/2018/2/23/17033316/ugly-delicious-fried-chicken-recap-season-1-episode-6.

12. George Embiricos, "Meet the Man Who Launched the Nashville Hot Chicken Craze," Food Republic, August 25, 2016, https://www.foodrepublic.com/2016/08/25/meet-the-man-who-launched-the-nashville-hot-chicken-craze.

13. Serena Dai, "Please Stop Writing Racist Restaurant Reviews," Eater, March 23, 2016, https://ny.eater.com/2016/3/23/11290082/stop-writing-racist-restaurant-reviews.

14. Dai, "Please Stop Writing Racist Restaurant Reviews."

15. Rajeev Balasubramanyam, "A Short Description of Cultural Appropriation for Non-Believers," *McSweeney's*, April 17, 2017, https://www.mcsweeneys.net/articles/a-short-description-of-cultural-appropriation-for-non-believers.

16. Michael W. Twitty, *The Cooking Gene: A Journey Through African-American Culinary History in the Old South* (New York: Amistad, 2017).

CHAPTER 8: THE ENTREPRENEUR

1. Steve Light, "Why 'Race Riot'? On the Need to Change a Misleading Term," *Blog// Los Angeles Review of Books*, November 12, 2016, https://blog.lareviewofbooks.org/essays/race-riot-need-change-misleading-term.

2. Chesnutt, *The Marrow of Tradition*; "From W. E. B. Du Bois," letter, reprinted in Chesnutt, *The Marrow of Tradition*.

3. Chesnutt, *The Marrow of Tradition*.

4. Wilmington Race Riot Commission, *1898 Wilmington Race Riot Report*, May 31, 2006, http://digital.ncdcr.gov/cdm/ref/collection/p249901coll22/id/5842.

5. Victor Luckerson, "Black Wall Street: The African American Haven That Burned and Then Rose from the Ashes," *Ringer*, June 28, 2018, https://www.theringer.com/2018/6/28/17511818/black-wall-street-oklahoma-greenwood-destruction-tulsa.

6. Kevin Schultz, "Pot for Your Pup? Startups Cash In on Cannabis Trend," *San Francisco Chronicle*, October 23, 2015, https://www.sfchronicle.com/business/article/Pot-for-your-pup-Startups-cash-in-on-cannabis-6587018.php#photo-8815338.

7. "Alison Ettel CEO & Co-Founder, TreatWell," *Edibles Magazine*, March 14, 2016, https://ediblesmagazine.com/edibles/alison-ettel-ceo-co-founder-treatwell.

8. H. J. Anslinger, "Marijuana, Assassin of Youth," *American Magazine*, July 1937.

9. "Marijuana Traffic Rises, U.S. Aid [*sic*] Tells House Committee," *Chicago Daily Tribune*, March 2, 1949.

10. "Marijuana Traffic Rises."

11. "Hearings Before Subcommittee No. 5 on H.R. 140 [and Other] Miscellaneous Bills Regarding the Civil Rights of Persons Within the Jurisdiction of the United States" (Washington: GPO, 1957).

12. Larry Sloman, *Reefer Madness: The History of Marijuana in America* (Indianapolis: Bobbs Merrill, 1979).

13. On Anslinger's targeting of Billie Holiday, see Johann Hari, *Chasing the Scream: The First and Last Days of the War on Drugs* (New York: BloomsburyUSA, 2016).

14. German Lopez, "How Obama Quietly Reshaped America's War on Drugs," Vox, December 12, 2016, https://www.vox.com/identities/2016/12/19/13903532/obama-war-on-drugs-legacy.

15. Human Rights Watch, *Every 25 Seconds: The Human Toll of Criminalizing Drug Use in the United States*, October 12, 2016, https://www.hrw.org/report/2016/10/12/every-25-seconds/human-toll-criminalizing-drug-use-united-states.

16. Drug Policy Alliance, *From Prohibition to Progress: A Status Report on Marijuana Legalization*, January 22, 2018, http://www.drugpolicy.org/sites/default/files/dpa_marijuana_legalization_report_feb14_2018_0.pdf.

17. Drug Policy Alliance, *From Prohibition to Progress*; Human Rights Watch, *Every 25 Seconds*.

18. Anslinger, "Marijuana, Assassin of Youth."

19. US Drug Enforcement Administration, "Drug Scheduling," https://www.dea.gov/drug-scheduling, accessed April 24, 2019.

20. Niella Orr, "Weed, Whitewashed," *Baffler*, July 2015, https://thebaffler.com/salvos/weed-whitewashed.

21. Orr, "Weed, Whitewashed."

22. Amanda Mull, "The Sad News About CBD Cupcakes," *Atlantic*, January 15, 2019, https://www.theatlantic.com/health/archive/2019/01/cbd-food/580483.

23. US Department of Justice, Office of the Attorney General, "Department Policy on Charging Mandatory Minimum Sentences and Recidivist Enhancements in Certain Drug Cases," August 12, 2013, https://www.justice.gov/sites/default/files/ag/legacy/2014/04/11/ag-memo-drug-guidance.pdf.

24. US Department of Justice, Office of the Attorney General, "Department Charging and Sentencing Policy," May 10, 2017, https://www.justice.gov/opa/pr/attorney-general-sessions-issues-charging-and-sentencing-guidelines-federal-prosecutors.

25. White House, "Remarks by President Trump on the National Security and Humanitarian Crisis on Our Southern Border," briefing, February 15, 2019, https://www.whitehouse.gov/briefings-statements/remarks-president-trump-national-security-humanitarian-crisis-southern-border.

26. "Chart: Percentage of Cannabis Business Owners and Founders by Race," September 11, 2017, *Marijuana Business Daily*, https://mjbizdaily.com/chart-19-cannabis-businesses-owned-founded-racial-minorities.

27. Amanda Chicago Lewis, "America's Whites-Only Weed Boom," *BuzzFeed*, March 16, 2016, https://www.buzzfeednews.com/article/amandachicagolewis/americas-white-only-weed-boom.

28. City of Oakland, "Become an Equity Applicant or Incubator," http://www2.oaklandnet.com/government/o/CityAdministration/cannabis-permits/OAK068455, accessed April 12, 2019.

29. Ben Kesslen, "Baltimore Will No Longer Prosecute Marijuana Possession," *NBC News*, January 29, 2019.

30. Benjamin Goggin, "Black People Face Big Barriers Entering the Legal Weed Industry," September 20, 2018, https://free.vice.com/en_us/article/yw4pkw/weed -industry-equity-black-business.

31. Goggin, "Black People Face Big Barriers Entering the Legal Weed Industry."

32. Judith Ohikuare, "Can Black Women Do Good & Get Rich in Big Cannabis?" Refinery29, June 22, 2018, https://www.refinery29.com/en-us/2018/06 /195690/black-women-starting-cannabis-businesses.

33. Rina Cakrani, "The Racist Weed Industry," Whitman Wire, March 8, 2018, https://whitmanwire.com/opinion/2018/03/08/the-racist-weed-industry.

34. Lewis, "America's Whites-Only Weed Boom."

35. Dominic Holden, "It's Not About the Stoners," The Stranger, October 24, 2012, https://www.thestranger.com/seattle/its-not-about-the-stoners/Content ?oid=15084994.

36. Nick Sibilla, "Tennessee Has Fined Residents Nearly $100,000, Just for Braiding Hair," Forbes, March 13, 2018, https://www.forbes.com/sites/institutefor justice/2018/03/13/tennessee-has-fined-residents-nearly-100000-just-for-braiding -hair/#15cf524d174c.

37. Angela Wilson, "The Do's and Don'ts of Starting an Instagram Boutique," Source, May 29, 2015, http://thesource.com/2015/05/29/the-dos-and-donts-of -starting-an-instagram-boutique.

38. A 2016 study ("Black and White: Access to Capital Among Minority-Owned Startups," SIEPR Discussion Paper No. 17-03, Stanford University Institute for Economic Policy Research, December 15, 2016) conducted by economists Robert Fairlie (University of California, Santa Cruz) et al. found that white businesses started with an average of $106,702 in capital, compared to $35,205 for black-owned businesses.

39. Jenna Wortham, "Instagram's TMZ," New York Times Magazine, April 14, 2015, https://www.nytimes.com/2015/04/19/magazine/instagrams-tmz.html.

40. Doree Shafrir, "The Shade Room Is Coming for the Gossip Industry's Wig," BuzzFeed, December 15, 2015, https://www.buzzfeed.com/doree/how-the-shade -room-is-changing-celebrity-gossip.

CHAPTER 9: THE ACTIVIST

1. Mikki Kendall, "#SolidarityIsForWhiteWomen: Women of Color's Issue with Digital Feminism," Guardian, August 14, 2013, https://www.theguardian.com /commentisfree/2013/aug/14/solidarityisforwhitewomen-hashtag-feminism.

2. Kendall, "#SolidarityIsForWhiteWomen."

3. John Eligon, "Michael Brown Spent Last Weeks Grappling with Problems and Promise," New York Times, August 24, 2014, https://www.nytimes.com/2014/08 /25/us/michael-brown-spent-last-weeks-grappling-with-lifes-mysteries.html.

4. P. Khalil Saucier and Tryon P. Woods, "Introduction: Racial Optimism and the Drag of Thymotics," in Conceptual Aphasia in Black: Displacing Racial Formation, ed. Saucier and Woods (Lanham, MD: Lexington Books, 2018).

5. Audre Lorde, A Burst of Light: Essays (Ann Arbor: Firebrand Books, 1988).

6. Aisha Harris, "A History of Self-Care," Slate, April 5, 2017, http://www.slate .com/articles/arts/culturebox/2017/04/the_history_of_self_care.html.

7. Jonathan M. Metzl, *The Protest Psychosis: How Schizophrenia Became a Black Disease* (Boston: Beacon Press, 2009).

8. Metzl, *The Protest Psychosis*.

CONCLUSION: BUSINESS AS USUAL

1. Walter Benn Michaels, "Nobody's Story: The Myth of Cultural Appropriation," *Chronicle of Higher Education*, July 7, 2017, https://www.chronicle.com/article/The-Myth-of-Cultural/240464.